AN HOUR
At HOME

dedication. To my grandmothers, Alice and Elizabeth, who touched many lives — especially mine.

AN HOUR *At* HOME

Text and photography by

SUe STUBBS

MURDOCH BOOKS

CONTENTS

INTRODUCTION

HERITAGE

My mother once said to me, 'We grew up recycling and reusing, but it didn't have a name, then — we did it because we had to.'

My grandmother kept a large basket of wool in the living room containing all the leftover balls and scraps from knitted jumpers. Jumpers the grandkids had outgrown had also been unpicked and unravelled so the wool could be re-used. It was saved for knitting brightly coloured tea cosies for school fetes, stuffed animals and squares that were joined together to make knee rugs and blankets that were donated to charities.

During rainy school holidays, Nana taught the girls to knit squares and scarves, to do fancywork (embroidery) and crochet the edges of cotton and linen hankies. The oak table, which was used for family gatherings, was where we learnt to iron tea towels, arrange flowers we picked from the garden, sew hems on linen tablecloths, repair sheets that needed to be turned and embellish straw hats for festivities. It was also where we sat to watch Nana decorate cakes.

For many years it looked as though homemaking would pass me by, as I concentrated on travel and career. It wasn't until after the birth of my children that I began to realise how much I had learnt during my childhood, and saw that those skills now had a place in my life.

SIMPLICITY

The modern homemaker often juggles the demands of work and home, and home can become hectic and chaotic, rather than a sanctuary. Keep homemaking manageable by keeping it simple. For example, we tend to over-sanitise and over-clean, using a myriad of poisonous chemicals. Simple products and regular habits are enough to keep a house clean. Included in this book are recipes for cleaning products that will help keep your home chemical-free.

BASICS

Learning the basics — for example, which glue or thread or paint or stitch to use — and a few simple skills will allow you to tackle a multitude of projects. In this book, there is a list of what you need at the beginning of each project so you won't find yourself getting halfway through and realising you can't complete it because you don't have what you need.

TIME

Nowadays, most people don't have unlimited time to spend on homemaking, but small changes and projects can make a big difference. It is just as easy to make a cushion cover as it is to shop for one, and much more satisfying.

Breaking down larger projects into the separate steps involved will enable you to transform a corner, or an area, or a whole room using the chunks of time you have available. Even a spare five minutes can be used to do a simple task, or complete a small part of a larger project.

And in the flurry of modern life, time spent making your home a haven is well worthwhile.

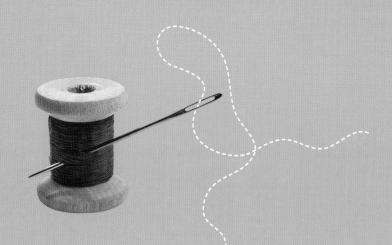

TAKEN TO TASK

TIPS FOR SUCCESSFUL
HOME MAINTENANCE

HOME MAINTENANCE KITS

When it comes to tackling household tasks, a little bit of organisation can work wonders. Simply keeping the basic materials together in the form of a kit will make any task or project easier to tackle successfully.

These kits are intended as a guide to the basics only. As you use the kits for cleaning, sewing, painting and so on, you will discover your own specific requirements. Add to a kit any extra elements that suit your needs. Check and amend the kits often, but keep them simple and pared back, free from surplus.

Be creative when finding suitable containers for kits. I keep my mending kit in a beautiful old perfume box, my sewing kit in a fishing basket, and my craft kit in a painted box. Whatever you use, make sure that all elements of the kit are easily accessible.

Store the kits in appropriate places that are easy to get to — this way you will be more inclined to use them and to stay organised. The cleaning kit could be kept at the bottom of a broom cupboard, or in a bucket hanging from a hook in the laundry. You might have a suitable cupboard in the back room or shed or under the stairs for the painting kit. Or it may be that you have a specific cupboard where all the kits can be stored together.

CLEANING KIT

Having everything you need in one place will make any cleaning task quicker and easier. A cleaning kit should contain everything you need to do a basic clean of the inside of the home. Keep everything together in a container that is easy to carry from room to room, preferably one with a handle, like a bucket or basket. Store the kit in the laundry or kitchen, together with a mop and a soft-bristled broom. On the day you're cleaning, toss in a lemon — one of the most useful cleaning ingredients in the kitchen.

Lined rubber gloves or disposable gloves allow you to use hotter water temperatures without burning your hands, and will prevent skin irritations.

Bicarbonate of soda is slightly alkaline, and absorbs odours. It is a good, non-abrasive cleaner for walls, kitchen bench tops, bathroom tiles and other non-greasy bathroom surfaces. For tiles and kitchen benches, mix into a paste with a little water, apply with a damp cloth, leave on for a few minutes, then rinse. Use a clean, damp cloth to wipe off any residual

A PASTE OF BICARBONATE OF SODA AND WATER HAS MANY CLEANING USES

bicarbonate of soda. For more stubborn marks, such as those found in a bath, dip a damp cloth into the powder and use directly on the grime. For crystal and glassware, and for walls, mix $\frac{1}{4}$ cup into 1 litre of warm water.

Small container and mixing spoon for mixing up bicarbonate of soda paste.

Washing soda (sodium carbonate) is more strongly alkaline than bicarbonate of soda, and will give a better result in areas where there is more grime. It cuts grease and oils, and is good for cleaning sinks and tubs, especially ceramic and stainless steel. Use in the same way you would use bicarbonate of soda. Be careful when using it, though, as it can cause skin irritations. Do not use on aluminium.

White vinegar kills bacteria, mould and germs, and is useful in the bathroom and laundry. Don't worry about the smell of the vinegar, as it dissipates after a couple of hours.

Detergent Use detergents that are environmentally friendly, and use them sparingly—it's easy to get into the habit of using excess, but often only a small amount is required.

Essential oils Lavender, tea tree and eucalyptus oils all have disinfectant qualities and give the home a fresh scent.

Essential oils — when diluted with water and shaken well — can be used as a room spray, for washing a timber floor or for wiping down the bathroom basin and tiles. A few drops in the final rinse of the washing machine will keep laundry and linens smelling fresh.

Shoe polish — brown and neutral. Shoe polish makes a great cover-up for scratches on leather, wooden furniture or timber floors. Neutral shoe polish works for buffing wooden furniture, whether painted or waxed.

Salt has a slight abrasiveness and is useful for cleaning tea stains from cups. Use an old toothbrush dipped in salt to clean tile grout.

Lint-free cloths for dusting, wiping and polishing — when the cloths have gone through the wash, pop them straight back into the kit.

Brushes Keep a selection of scrubbing and dusting brushes. Paintbrushes can be used for dusting computer keyboards and delicate, intricate details such as those found on antique furniture or ornaments. An old toothbrush can be used to clean tile grout and hard-to-get-at areas such as behind the basin taps.

SEWING KIT

Whether it's for a quick hand-stitching task or a more complicated dressmaking project, having all sewing requirements in one basket or box will make any project easier to tackle.

A small fishing basket makes a great sewing kit. But a small box such as a shoe box, painted or covered, will also work well; or you could use a small, inexpensive set of craft wood drawers.

Within the kit, small plastic ziplock bags are useful for storing threaded bobbins and embroidery thread. A collection of small containers will hold safety pins and dressmaking pins, buttons and small embellishments such as beads.

Pins and needles When buying pins and needles, it's a good idea to purchase a good brand name, as the quality can vary, and sewing with a blunt needle can prove tiresome and frustrating. You will need a variety of sewing needles of different sizes for tasks ranging from delicate hand stitching through to embroidery. Needles are often available in variety packs.

Sewing machine needles

Thread — a selection of colours Include the basic colours such as black, white, cream, grey, blue, red and green. You will also need to buy thread as you plan your projects. Use good quality thread, as it is more resistant to snapping and to wear and tear in the completed project.

Pincushion A simple pincushion is easy to make — see the instructions on page 63.

Thimble Thimbles save the fingertips, and are particularly useful when pushing a needle through a resistant fabric or leather.

Magnet for picking up pins and needles Alternatively, keep a magnet on the sewing machine and, as you pull the pins out while sewing, pop them onto the magnet.

Dressmaking scissors Sharp scissors make all the difference! Buy the best quality you can afford, and have them sharpened regularly. Keep the scissors specifically for cutting fabric, so they don't become blunt.

Pinking shears or zigzag scissors These are used less frequently, but need to be kept sharp. Keep them in a protective case, as otherwise the tips can become blunt, making cutting difficult.

Thread clippers For short and delicate threads, scissors can be cumbersome, and thread clippers are quick and easy to use.

Fray stopper stops edges of cloth fraying. Available from craft stores.

Elastic Include fine hat elastic and 5 mm elastic.

Fabric marker Washable fabric markers are great — but not all projects will be washed after they're made (particularly if the fabric has been pre-washed to shrink first). In this case, use light-sensitive pens that fade under UV light, or chalk that brushes out.

Safety pins Various sizes

Tape measure Plastic tape measures are the most common, but can stretch, so take care not to roll them too tightly, and don't leave them in a sunny spot, as the heat can warp them.

Steel ruler A steel ruler won't stretch, shrink or warp, and this makes it the most accurate measuring tool.

Set square This helps to line up 90 degree corners accurately.

Tracing paper Keep a few sheets of tracing paper tucked into the sewing kit — it makes copying and tracing designs simple.

TIP. To stop the thread unravelling from a reel of cotton, use a piece of Blu-tack the size of a match head to hold the end of the thread in place. Alternatively, wrap an elastic band around the reel to hold the loose end down. This will guarantee fewer tangles in the sewing kit, and it will be easier to take out individual reels.

MENDING KIT

A mending kit is basically a smaller version of a sewing kit, with a few other tricks. It's what you use for minor or emergency repairs — the box you pull out when you need a safety pin, or need to fix a hem, sew on a button, glue on a label, cut off a thread, or write a child's name on an ID tag. A mending kit can feel like a lifesaver in last-minute situations.

   The kit can be kept in a small tin or box. Whatever you use, keep it simple and make sure all materials are easily accessible.

Needles and thread Include only the most common colours of thread used for buttons and hems — white, grey, blue and black will generally do at a pinch.

Iron-on hemming tape Include a small amount of black and white hemming tape for emergencies. It also makes a great, effective iron-on patch for a small area.

Buttons Include just the most common — for example, shirt buttons and buttons for the cushions and doona cover.

Dressmaking pins

Safety pins

Pincushion

Masking tape will pick up any last minute fluff or loose threads. Tear off approximately 20 cm and wrap it around your palm and knuckles. Tap the threads with your knuckles, and the loose threads will stick to the tape.

Clear nail polish will prevent knits from running, and cloth from fraying.

Superglue for emergency repairs

Craft or paper glue

Small, sharp, multipurpose scissors

Fine permanent maker for writing on lunchboxes, labels, plastic and paper

CRAFT KIT

Keep a few craft tools together in a tool box or a plastic storage container with a fitted lid. Tools are best kept separate from craft materials — for example, paints, inks, cardboard, ribbons and shells — so that they don't get lost among the materials. Store craft materials in separate plastic takeaway containers. Clear containers allow you to see what's in them, and food containers are generally a good size to hold all the 'bits'. If you are not using transparent containers, group similar items together — for example, ribbons or buttons — and label the boxes.

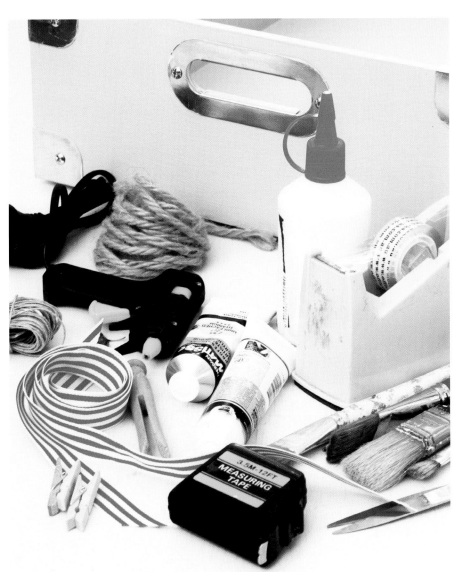

Craft knife Blades need to be sharp for accurate cutting and, depending on what you're cutting, they can become blunt quite quickly, so include a few extra blades. Keep the blade safely pulled in, or a protective cover over the tip.

Steel ruler for measuring, and — when used with a sharp craft knife — for cutting accurately

Pencils Have a selection of lead pencils and coloured pencils handy.

PVA glue Include a good quality general purpose glue that dries clear.

Spray adhesive Repositionable spray adhesive will give a thin mist of glue — perfect when working with paper and card. It has a slower drying time, and is tacky enough for items to be lifted up and placed again.

Hot glue gun and glue sticks These glue most surfaces and objects.

Scissors Include sharp paper scissors with good quality tips for cutting sharp corners.

String Keep a few types of string or cord handy. Great for bundling things together.

Stapler

PAINTING KIT

Painting is not something you are likely do every day, but you may find that once you get started on a project, you are more likely to do a couple of painting tasks while you're at it. Keep brushes and rollers clean, well-maintained and stored, and they will always be ready to use. To keep painting gear organised, separate it into a couple of clear plastic stackable boxes. Keep one box for preparation materials — sandpaper, sanding blocks, drop sheets and masking tape — and another box for painting and clean-up, with rollers, brushes, openers and stirrers, cling wrap, small buckets and clean rags or cloths. You'll be able to find what you need for each job much more easily.

Paintbrushes You'll need a selection of brushes in your kit. Include a cutting-in brush, and 25 mm (1 in), 50 mm (2 in) and 100 mm (4 in) brushes. Buy good quality brushes, and take care of them — it's easier to get a good paint finish using a quality brush in good condition. See Cleaning and Caring for Paintbrushes and Rollers, pages 38–41, for more information.

Drop sheets Old bed sheets make great drop sheets, providing they are not torn. They won't prevent spills soaking through, but a little caution will minimise accidents. The larger, heavyweight drop sheets are more durable and will stop spills soaking through. Plastic disposable drop sheets are great for one-offs or emergencies, but are not very durable.

Roller and tray A short nap roller is multipurpose and will do most regular painting jobs, for example walls. For anything specialised, you may need other rollers. Plastic trays are inexpensive.

Paint can openers have an easy-to-hold handle, which means less risk of the tin slipping and the paint spilling. Don't be tempted to use screwdrivers to open paint tins — it will damage them and make them useless.

Paint stirrer Paint requires a good stirring so that all the pigments are mixed in. Don't shake the can of paint, as this creates air bubbles, particularly if the tin is not full. A paint stirrer needs to be wide and flat and easy to clean.

Small bucket When using large tins of paint, rather than keeping the whole can exposed to air and dust, pour a smaller amount into a small bucket. This prevents waste, and if the bucket is knocked over there will only be a small amount to clean up. This strategy is also useful when painting small, fiddly projects.

Wire brush for cleaning paintbrushes, and for removing loose and flaking paint and rust from metal surfaces.

Masking tape 2.5 cm masking tape will mask off most areas. Don't leave masking tape on any longer than the manufacturer recommends, as it will stick fast and be very difficult to get off. It may also pull off the paint you had masked.

Cling wrap If you need to put the brush or roller down for a few minutes, wrap the brush or roller in cling wrap to stop the paint from drying out. This will work for a few hours if the brush or roller is wrapped tightly. When closing a tin of paint, place a layer of cling wrap over the paint surface to help prolong the life of the paint.

Clean rags Include a selection of lint-free cotton cloths. Wipe over-painted areas with a dry cloth first, and if paint remains, use a damp cloth. Keep a damp cloth nearby to wipe up small spills around the paint can and for wiping paint off fingers. Wipe any splatters off ladders immediately using a dry cloth, as paint splatters or a damp cloth can cause a ladder to be slippery. After washing brushes and

USING THE CORRECT TOOL TO OPEN PAINT TINS IS EASIER AND SAFER

shaking out excess water, pat them dry with a dry rag.

Rubber bands are useful for paint brush storage. Roll the bristles of the brush in a thick layer of brown paper or newspaper, then put a rubber band around the brush to hold. Don't allow the rubber band to sit over the bristles, as it may push them out of shape. When you have finished the painting for a project, slide a rubber band onto the paint tin at the level the paint comes to. When you need to know how much paint you have left in a particular colour, the level will be marked.

T I P. If you don't have a paint stirrer, use a flat stick or piece of timber off-cut. Stir gently to lessen the air bubbles that can get trapped in the paint, which are difficult to get rid of, and gently scrape the bottom of the tin. The pigments tend to settle on the bottom and this helps mix them in. Stir paint for at least a few minutes to mix thoroughly.

BASIC TOOL KIT

Unless you are the home handyman or the local DIY person, your tool box doesn't need to resemble the local hardware store — you just need a few basic tools, and a small tool box to house them. A basic tool kit is invaluable when you need to hammer in a loose nail, tighten a screw on a cupboard handle or drill a hole to hang a picture.

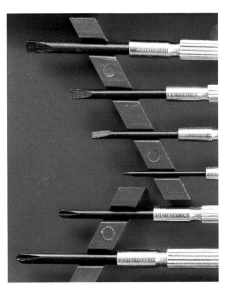

SCREWS VARY IN LENGTH, THICKNESS, THREAD AND HEAD SHAPE

THE MOST COMMON SCREWDRIVER TYPES: PHILLIPS HEAD AND SLOTTED TIP

JEWELLERS' SCREWDRIVERS ARE IDEAL FOR VERY SMALL SCREWS

Screwdrivers come in a variety of sizes to match those of screws. Keep a couple of sizes of each of the slotted tip and Phillips head screwdrivers, which are the most common. Good quality tips don't break as easily, and are worth spending a little extra on. Include a set of jewellers' screwdrivers — these will tighten a loose screw on the sewing machine, or the tiny screws in the arms of glasses — and Allen keys.

Hammer Include a basic claw hammer for hitting in nails.

Selection of screws and nails There are many kinds available (including those for special purposes, for example for use with plaster or masonry, or roofing nails, which are galvanised), but you will just need a basic selection — a small handful of each of three or four different sizes, from small to medium. When selecting a nail or screw, measure the length needed. If it is too long, the tip may appear where it's not wanted;

too short, and it won't hold the pieces together. Screws and nails are also available in variety packs. You should find everything you need in a variety pack, but if in doubt ask the salesperson for help.

Flat nose pliers and needle nose (or pointy) pliers are the most common and useful hand tools for gripping.

Multigrips (not pictured) Multigrip locking pliers have adjustable jaws useful for gripping and twisting. They also have wider jaws than normal pliers. If you have difficulty removing the knobs from the stove, they are good for this and other similar jobs.

Power drill — corded or cordless A plug-in corded drill is less expensive and generally gives a better performance than a cordless drill. You won't have the batteries go flat at a crucial moment—but you will probably need an extension power lead. Batteries for cordless drills don't have a

HANDY HINT.

When using pliers or multigrips to hold anything that might scratch, cover the object first with a soft cotton cloth or a chamois. This will prevent the jaws from scratching the item they are gripping.

Using a magnetic tip screwdriver will help you avoid dropping the screw, as it will stick to the magnet.

long shelf life and, when in use, may not give the power required. If you use the drill infrequently, the batteries' charging capacity is reduced, giving a shorter usage time before they go flat. But for small projects where it's a matter of, say, putting a screw into a wall, a cordless is ideal.

Sandpaper Include a few sheets of various grades of sandpaper.

CLEANING AND MAINTENANCE

It can be easy to feel caught up in a never-ending cleaning cycle — no sooner is the cleaning done than the process needs to start again. However, there are ways to make cleaning easier and less of a chore.

Keep cleaning materials all together in one place — see the Cleaning Kit on page 13 for ideas — and keep them simple. Often one product will do for many tasks, for example bicarbonate of soda will work for the kitchen bench, for the bathtub, and for rugs. Try to use natural products, so that fewer chemicals accumulate within the home.

It's useful to have a chamois for polishing glass, and a microfibre cloth, but for general purpose cleaning rags you can cut up old towels or cotton household linens such as old sheets, as was done traditionally. Re-using materials is good for the environment — and your budget! The rags can be discarded once they're no longer effective. For hygiene reasons, keep cleaning cloths separate by colour coding them. Use different colours for kitchen, bathroom and laundry.

Keep cleaning tasks simple, too. If you have little available time, try breaking large tasks down into smaller tasks that are easier to tackle.

CLEANING WET AREAS

THE KITCHEN

One of the most useful cleaning ingredients in the kitchen is lemon. It has antibacterial qualities and a fresh and invigorating scent. It also acts as a whitener/bleach.

Another useful natural product is bicarbonate of soda, which is excellent for deodorising drains or the fridge, and for cleaning metal surfaces such as aluminium and stainless steel. As the bicarb is alkaline, it removes or cuts through grease and grime. It works as a deodoriser by absorbing smells rather than masking them. If you have any concerns about it scratching a soft surface, test a small area first.

  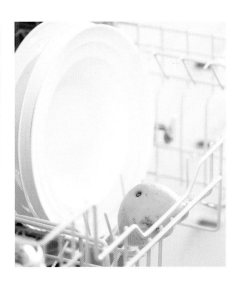

CUTTING BOARD

Use one half of a cut lemon. Dip the cut side in coarse-grained cooking salt and rub onto the wooden cutting board or scrubbed pine table. It will deodorise, act as an antibacterial agent and bleach the timber. To keep the timber of the board from drying out and splitting, after the salt rub dip the cut side of the lemon into olive oil and rub over the board again. Allow a couple of hours for the oil to penetrate before using the board again.

FRIDGE

Wipe the fridge clean with a solution of bicarbonate of soda mixed with warm water. To keep the fridge smelling fresh, wipe the inside of the fridge with vanilla essence after cleaning. This will banish any fridge or freezer smells. Alternatively, place an opened box of bicarbonate of soda in the fridge — this will absorb any odours.

DISHWASHER

Pop one half of a lemon onto a prong in the dishwasher. The oils in the skin of the lemon will be extracted with the heat of the water and mix with the water spray of the dishwasher. The lemon will freshen and scent the dishwasher and will have no ill effect on the dishes. It will do a few washes over a couple of days. The lemon can be stored in the fridge between washes, carefully identified so it's not mistaken for an edible lemon.

TIP. Cut up old towels to use as cleaning cloths. About 20 cm (8 in) square is an ideal size for cleaning and polishing.

STEP 1

STEP 2

STEP 3

USE A SOFT CLOTH TO BUFF AND
POLISH STAINLESS STEEL

HAN**dy** H**i**NT.

Put 500 ml of water and a few slices of lemon into a microwave-proof jug. Microwave on high for a few minutes, then allow it to sit in the microwave for at least five minutes. The steam will soften any tough stains or spilled food. Wipe clean with an absorbent cloth.

STOVE

The stove top tends to become a repository for all kinds of grease and spilled food. Cleaning as you go will prevent the clean-up turning into a mammoth task involving hours of soaking and scrubbing. Only clean the stove when it's turned off. Use a microfibre cloth to wipe up all spills, and rinse the cloth after each use.

It's not advisable to use abrasives on any stove top surface, as scratching will occur. Mix a paste of bicarbonate of soda and water and apply this to any hardened spills. Allow to soak, then wipe the stove over. (If you have any concerns about it scratching a surface, test a small area first.) For stainless steel, be sure to clean or rub with the grain. Polish stainless steel and enamel with a soft cloth.

Clean the splashback with a microfibre cloth, using a small amount of detergent. Rinse with a clean damp cloth, then polish dry.

For removable parts, follow the steps below.

STEP 1 For a more thorough clean, take off all removable parts first and soak them in hot water and detergent. Clean cast iron trivets using a scourer or small scrubbing brush. If the stove has knobs that pull off, these can also be soaked and washed in hot water and detergent.

STEP 2 Rinse removable parts in hot water.

STEP 3 Place cast iron parts on a towel or cloth to dry, as they will scratch a soft surface. Make sure they are completely dry before replacing them, as otherwise they can cause rust stains.

THE LAUNDRY

Laundry appliances are costly to replace, but following the manufacturer's instructions for regular cleaning and maintenance will increase their longevity. It takes only a few moments to wipe excess moisture away or clean a lint filter.

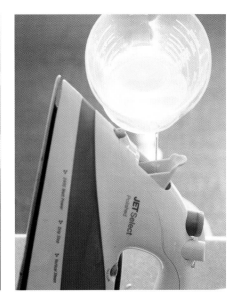

WASHING MACHINE

You can buy commercial antibacterial products for deodorising your linen and the washing machine — but a simple and effective way of treating both at the same time is to simply add a few drops of eucalyptus oil to 500 ml of water, and pour this into the final rinse when washing linens.

It's a good idea to occasionally run the machine through a cycle without any garments or linen. Add 2 cups of vinegar or half a cup of household bleach as the machine is filling. This will clean and deodorise the machine, and prevent waste building up in hard-to-get-at places.

TUMBLE DRYER

Clean the lint filter regularly. Get into the habit of cleaning it out either before or after each dryer load. Keeping the filter clean makes the dryer more efficient — and also reduces the risk of fire.

When the dryer is not in use, place inside it a small cloth with a few drops of lavender oil sprinkled onto it. The scent will stay in the dryer for the next time it's used. Remember to take the cloth out before you next use the dryer.

IRON

Use distilled water in the iron, as this will prevent hard minerals from calcifying and clogging the spray nozzles. Emptying the iron of water after each use will prevent a build-up of dirt that can cause the iron to spit sooty water.

Use lavender linen water in the iron (see Simple Household Recipes, page 42), or you can keep it in a spray bottle to spray on linen when ironing.

TIP. Keep the laundry dust-free, well-ventilated and dry. Wipe down any condensation or moisture that occurs when using the tumble dryer, open doors and windows if possible, and allow the room to dry out. This will prevent dampness and mould. Don't store damp laundry in closed baskets or buckets — wash and dry it as soon as possible.

THE BATHROOM

The shower is an area of the bathroom that tends to accumulate grime and soap scum. A microfibre cloth will remove most of the soap without the addition of chemicals, but a small amount of detergent, vinegar or lemon juice — or a combination of detergent and vinegar — will help to remove the scum build-up.

STEP 1

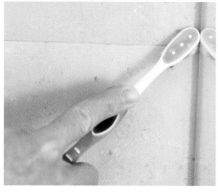

STEP 2

STEP 3

HAND BASIN

This is the most frequently used area of the bathroom. Chrome taps and spouts become watermarked quickly, and need to be wiped down frequently. To give your bathroom a quick pick-me-up, wipe over the hand basin spout and taps with a lint-free polishing cloth. Add a fresh soap and a handtowel with a couple of sprigs of lavender laid on top, give the mirror a quick wipe, and the bathroom will appear instantly fresh and clean.

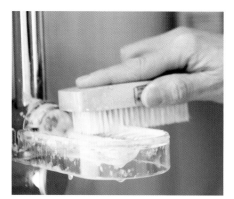

STEP 4

STEP 5

STEP 1   Wet the surface with water, then sprinkle on bicarbonate of soda, or spray on vinegar and detergent solution — see Simple Household Recipes, page 47.

STEP 2   Wipe the shower over with a microfibre cloth. Use an old toothbrush to scrub the grout and hard-to-get-at corners.

STEP 3   Polish taps, shower head and all metal surfaces by wiping down with a microfibre cloth, using a small amount of bicarbonate of soda if necessary.

STEP 4   Use a grooming nail brush to scrub soap-holders, as the bristles are a little softer than those of regular scrubbing brushes and tend not to scratch. Once soap scum has been removed, rinse thoroughly.

STEP 5   Wipe down any glass, including doors, then use a chamois to polish.

CLEANING DRY AREAS

In the dry areas of the house — for example, the living room, dining room and bedroom—carpets, rugs and furnishings all attract dust and dust mites. It is important to dust, sweep and vacuum regularly, and to keep these rooms as fresh and well-ventilated as possible.

STEP 1

STEP 2

STEP 3

CARPETED FLOORS AND RUGS

Rugs and wall-to-wall carpets collect dust, and therefore dust mites. They need to be cleaned regularly using a vacuum cleaner or carpet sweeper. Where possible, take smaller rugs outside to air, but keep them out of direct sunlight as they may fade.

To deodorise and clean the carpet or rug, mix bicarbonate of soda with a few drop of a citrus essential oil and sprinkle it on. Use an old flour sifter to sprinkle the mix evenly. Leave it for a few hours if possible, then thoroughly vacuum or sweep. Avoid walking on the rug until it's been vacuumed, so as to avoid separating the fibres.

TIMBER AND TILED FLOORS

Timber and tiled floors need to be swept regularly as grit that is walked underfoot will scratch the surface. Dirt and dust should be cleaned off the floor before it is washed.

STEP 1 Use a soft broom or a microfibre cloth or mop that traps the dust. Collect the pile of dust with a small dustpan and brush.

STEP 2 Wipe the floor over with eucalyptus cleaning solution (see Simple Household Recipes, page 47), using a well wrung-out mop. The drier the mop, the more effectively it will clean. Also, excess water can damage the tile or timber by seeping under the surface. Spot clean any visible marks or spills by wiping with a cloth.

STEP 3 Clean the mop by picking off any lint, then rinsing the mop in hot water.

HANDY HINT.

Dust often collects on the floor between regular cleaning times. To get rid of dust quickly, place a damp microfibre cloth over the end of the broom, using elastic bands to hold the cloth in place. Use the broom to mop away the dust — it will collect on the end of the cloth. Give the cloth a good shake outside before throwing it into the wash.

OPEN WINDOWS AND DOORS

MAKE USE OF NATURAL LIGHT

PLANTS IMPROVE AIR QUALITY

HANDY HINT.

A teaspoon of sugar added to the water of most cut flowers will prolong their life. The sugar becomes food for the flower stems, allowing them to live longer. A small amount of household bleach can also be added. This will prevent bacteria from destroying the stem and making the water smelly. Change the water every couple of days.

ROOM VENTILATION AND FRESHNESS

Good cross-ventilation will move air out of trapped areas, rejuvenating the whole house. But not all residences have good cross-ventilation, or are light and airy, so it becomes important to take measures not to allow the air to become stale. There is something very purifying about having fresh air moving through a house—so throw the windows and doors open on a spring day, even if there is a chill in the air.

Louvres are useful for ventilation control. You can determine the amount they open, and the direction in which they open, so they can be used to keep dust at bay and ventilation at the level you require.

Healthy plants contribute to the oxygenating of the environment and can certainly help a room look fresh. Remember to dust plants every now and then as well as watering them.

Flowers—from a single cut stem to a large arrangement—can add freshness to a room and bring it to life with colour and scent. The variety of colours, shapes and textures available can be used to reflect seasonal changes.

WALLS AND DOORFRAMES

Painted walls and doorframes tend to attract children's dirty fingerprints and dirt from pets as well as dust.

STEP 1 Spray the wall with vinegar solution (1 part vinegar to 5 parts water) and allow it to sit for a few moments.

STEP 2 Wipe the wall over with an absorbent, heavy-duty cloth such as a piece of towel. Use white cloths, as occasionally dye from coloured cloth will bleed onto walls and stain them. This should remove dirt and grease. For heavier marks, use a stronger vinegar solution, or try undiluted vinegar — the smell will dissipate within a couple of hours.

For wallpaper — dust with a microfibre cloth that traps the dust (check the instructions that come with the cloth), then wipe over gently with a damp cloth.

For doorframes and doors — add a few drops of mild detergent to a litre of hot water, dampen a cloth with the solution and wipe over.

WINDOWS

If windows simply need a light clean, wipe them over with a damp chamois. This will remove fingerprints and smudges. If the windows are grimier — for example, if they're exposed to dust or pollution from a busy road — apply tea and glycerine mix (see Simple Household Recipes, page 47) using a spray bottle, wipe with a lint-free cloth to remove grime, then use a chamois to dry. For stubborn dirt and streaks, use vinegar and water (1 part vinegar to 5 parts water) with a few drops of detergent mixed in. Use a chamois to polish the glass when dry. Chamois cloths will dry glass without leaving streaks. Using newspapers can leave streaks, as the ink of the newsprint often marks the glass.

STEP 1

STEP 2

WIPING A WINDOW WITH A CHAMOIS

HANDY HINT.

When cleaning windows, open the window and clean the frame. This prevents it gathering grime that can hold on to water, and so helps stop rot setting in to the timber or paint. Use an old, clean paintbrush or dustpan brush to loosen and remove the dirt, then wipe over with a damp microfibre cloth with some mild detergent added. Don't use abrasives on paintwork, as they will scratch the paint surface. Avoid bleach-based cleaners as well, as they cause paint to deteriorate.

SPOT-TEST ALL PRODUCTS FIRST

USE PURE SOAPS WITH NATURAL OILS

APPLY POLISH WITH A LINT-FREE CLOTH

HANDY HINT.

Keeping leather well-maintained and polished will minimise scratches, mould growth and general wear and tear. Leather, like timber, develops a patina as it ages and doesn't always need the full polish routine. Often just a quick buff with a soft cloth will polish and protect the surface and enhance appearance. When selecting a polish, choose one that's not oily or soft, as it may stain the leather. Always test a small area first.

LEATHER MAINTENANCE

Leather is a natural product, and will last for many years if well-maintained. It comes in a large variety of types and finishes, which vary in their ability to absorb oils — and there are just as many recommended ways to clean leather and keep it oiled and polished.

Leather used for furnishing is not subjected to dirt and the weather in the same way as saddlery leather, and so doesn't need to be treated in the same way. Upholstery leather is also often not as robust, and it will not tolerate cleaning products that saddlery leather will.

There are some general precautions and measures that can be taken to keep leather in good condition. Leather needs to be kept out of direct sunlight, as exposure to light will dry out its natural oils, causing it to harden and crack. Clean leather by wiping it down with a damp cloth — the cloth should first be wet, then squeezed out so that it is almost dry. Avoid using detergents or other chemical products where possible — these can change the natural composition of the leather, causing deterioration.

If necessary, you could rub the damp cloth over a bar of pure soap before applying it gently to the leather. Test the soap on a small area of leather that is out of sight first. Wipe over any marks, then wipe up any soap residue. There shouldn't be any soap bubbles, as this indicates too much water has been used. Wipe up any spills immediately, as leather will often stain if it gets wet.

When using any leather cleaning product, it's advisable to follow the manufacturers' instructions for both the leather and the cleaning product. If you haven't used the product before, test it first on a small area that is out of sight. It is all too easy to wipe over a whole cushion, then realise the product has caused staining.

To protect leather, use a natural beeswax polish — you'll find there are many available commercially. The beeswax nourishes and protects the leather. Use sparingly, so as not to build up excess wax that will become tacky and hold dust and grime.

MATTRESSES AND BED LINEN

Turn mattresses regularly. When vacuuming bedrooms, give the mattress a good vacuum as well. Take off all linen, mattress protectors and electric blankets first. Clean around the tucks and stitching lines in particular, as these are places dust tends to lodge.

Where affordable, use quality cotton bed sheets. Freshly laundered cotton sheets have a freshness that cannot be equalled by polyester bed linen. Pure cotton and linen need ironing to look, feel and smell their best, but try this shortcut. Allow the sheet to dry folded in half over the clothes line. Then unpeg and fold in half along the line by bringing the left side over to meet the right side. Join the corners together, and shake out any creases. Repeat a couple more times until you have a folded strip of sheet hanging over the clothes line. Give it a good shake and flatten the folds. Gently pull off the line and fold in the other direction. This will give you an almost wrinkle-free sheet to float over the bed the next time it is made.

BLANKETS

Woollen and mohair blankets need little looking after other than washing and airing. (Avoid dry cleaning where possible, as the chemicals used tend to leave residues.) It's a good idea to wash blankets after summer storage and before packing away for the winter. Wash by machine in warm water if you have a hand-wash cycle. Otherwise, wash the blankets in the bathtub or laundry sink. Dissolve wool wash in enough warm water to cover the blanket (see pages 45 and 46 for wool wash recipes). Add the blanket and allow to soak for 30 minutes — this will help loosen oils and dirt. Gently swish the blanket around to remove the dirt, and rinse two or three times to ensure all the oils are removed. Place a few extra drops of eucalyptus or tea tree oil in the water in the final rinse, to deter moths. Roll the blanket in towels to squeeze the water out, and hang on the clothesline.

FEATHER AND DOWN

Air feather and down pillows and doonas weekly by hanging them on the line or over a chair outside. Don't leave them out on a windy day, though, as they will collect dust. If you can't take pillows outside, put them in the tumble dryer for a few minutes on low — they will bounce back to life very quickly.

Feather and down items absorb our natural skin oils, so they need to be washed. Do this in summer, when the weather is warmer and the drying hours are longer. Dissolve pure soap flakes in water in the bathtub, then add the pillow or doona. Squeeze the water through gently, without allowing the feathers to clump. Rinse well in clean water a couple of times, adding a few drops of lavender to the final rinse. Squeeze excess water out by hand. More water can then be squeezed out of a doona by rolling it up tightly. Lay pillows flat on a towel, then roll the towel and pillow up together to squeeze out the water.

Hang pillows out to dry by pegging them to the clothesline by one end. The feathers will fall to the bottom, so shake them every few hours so that all the feathers will dry. Doonas need to be shaken every few hours to ensure even drying. If possible, line dry on a dry and breezy day with sunshine. Otherwise, dry the doona or pillow in a warm and well-ventilated place indoors, shaking the feathers more frequently. Then put it into the tumble dryer on a low setting (15 minutes for a pillow, and the same or a little longer for a doona) to fluff up the feathers and complete the drying. Check frequently that the feathers stay evenly distributed and don't bunch up, and don't allow the item to become hot, as it will damage the feathers or down.

AIR BED LINEN OUTDOORS IF YOU CAN

HANdY HINT.

When storing doonas for the winter, wrap loosely and place in a protective cotton bag, to allow ventilation. Anything plastic will hold moisture in, making the item smell of damp. Vacuum-pack space-saving bags will crush the feathers and down, making it flat and lifeless. Open cupboards that doonas are stored in frequently, to avoid musty smells.

STEP 1

STEP 2

STEP 3

KEEP BRASSO AWAY FROM THE FRAME

MIRRORS

Mirrors polish up well with bicarbonate of soda paste or toothpaste. If you use toothpaste, choose a basic kind — and not a gel toothpaste — as some toothpastes will leave a film on the glass.

STEP 1   Mix a tablespoon of bicarbonate of soda with enough water to make it into paste.

STEP 2   Use a damp cloth and a smear of the bicarbonate of soda paste or toothpaste and rub it over the mirror, then allow to dry.

STEP 3   Use a clean cloth to polish the mirror.

Brasso polish is slightly abrasive and is an effective cleaner for glass and mirrors. It seems to work particularly well with old mirrors. First, shake the Brasso container well. Use a clean, dry cloth to smear a film over the glass, then allow to dry. Polish with a soft dry cloth.

CRYSTAL ITEMS

Crystal is more delicate and porous than ordinary glassware and needs to be handled with a little extra care. Washing crystal in the dishwasher with very hot water and detergent can cause permanent clouding of the surface.

Wash crystal glasses and vases by hand in warm water—not hot. Line the sink or basin with a towel or rubber mat to minimise breakages. Don't hold glasses by the stem, as this can cause them to break. Add a few drops of detergent or soap flakes to the warm water and wash the glasses in the sudsy water. Go carefully, as the soap can make crystal glasses slippery. Rinse the glasses in a sinkful of warm water with approximately ½ cup of vinegar added for a sparkling finish. Wear gloves to avoid fingerprints. Allow the glasses to air dry.

When using crystal candle holders, remove the candle before it burns down to the holder (when it reaches about 3 cm above it), to prevent cracking. If wax spills on the holder, use hot water to soften it and remove it using your fingertips. Don't try scraping it with sharp tools, as this will scratch the crystal.

GLASSWARE

Glass is generally more robust than crystal. Recycled glass — although it appears to be robust — can be very fragile and needs to be treated with care. Pressed glass or depression glassware is prone to scratches, and it's best to avoid the dishwasher for all precious glassware where possible.

Glassware must be dried thoroughly as any moisture can leave stains which are almost impossible to remove. For bottles or vases that are difficult to clean, add a little bleach to hot water (not boiling) in the bottle or vase and either shake the bottle or rub the inside of the vase with a cloth. For more difficult grime, add rice or dried peas and shake or rub vigorously to loosen the dirt. Rinse thoroughly with water containing a little vinegar and dry with a lint-free cloth or leave to air dry.

To prevent vases from getting water marks, add a drop or two of detergent and a teaspoon of bleach. Top up with fresh water to change the water level, or change the water every couple of days.

DUST GLASSWARE REGULARLY

TIP. To remove coffee and tea stains from the inside of ceramic and china cups and teapots, dip the corner of a damp cotton cloth into coarse table or cooking salt (not rock salt). Rub the stain lightly until it disappears, then rinse well.

CLEANING AND CARING FOR PAINTBRUSHES AND ROLLERS

Buy the best quality brushes you can afford and care for them correctly, and you will have them to use over and over. Good brushes give a smoother finish and the paint will flow more evenly, making painting easier. And whether the bristles are natural or acrylic, brushes will last longer and give a better finish if well cared for.

Clean brushes as soon as possible after finishing, or at least soak them in water (for acrylic or water-based paints) or mineral turpentine or another appropriate solvent (for enamel paints). Don't allow the paint to dry on the brush. The longer you leave a brush to dry, the more the paint will harden, and the harder the task of cleaning the brush will be.

When the brush is loaded with paint, each bristle is coated with paint. It is essential to keep the bristles clean and not allow paint to build up on the bristles, particularly at the handle end. If a brush isn't cleaned correctly, paint will build up on the bristles as it ages, and eventually the bristles won't lie straight.

CRAFT BRUSHES NEED THE SAME CARE

BRUSHES LAST YEARS IF TREATED WELL

BE GENTLE WHEN USING A WIRE BRUSH

HANdY HiNT.

To remove dried paint from bristles, use a wire brush. Point the paint-brush downwards, resting the base on a hard surface such as the edge of the sink, and use the wire brush in downward strokes along the bristles. Be fairly gentle, as bristles tear easily. This should be used as a last resort, rather than as a regular cleaning method.

ENAMEL PAINTS

Don't allow enamel paint to dry on the brush, as it hardens and becomes impossible to remove. After using the paint, first wipe as much paint as possible off the brush with a dry rag. Soak the brush in a jar of mineral turpentine or another solvent such as paint thinner, making sure any remaining paint on the brush is covered with the solvent. Leave the brush to soak for a few hours, or overnight. Tap and swish the brush intermittently to dislodge the paint from the bristles.

After removing the brush from the jar of solvent and allowing any drips to fall back into the jar, wipe the brush with a clean rag. Wash the brush in warm water with a small amount of detergent added, taking care not to rub the bristles, but gently working the sudsy water between them. When all the solvent has been removed, rinse the brush in running water, and dry by first flicking out excess water, then using a rag to gently dry the bristles.

STEP 1

STEP 2

STEP 3

STEP 4

STEP 5

STEP 6

WATER-BASED OR ACRYLIC PAINTS

STEP 1 Rinse brushes in a container of water, or under running water. Don't turn brushes upside-down under running water, as this forces paint higher into the bristles. Rather than letting the water go down the drain, fill up a bucket that can be disposed of onto the garden.

STEP 2 Always dry the brush thoroughly by first flicking excess water out of it, then gently using a clean cloth to absorb the remaining water. To remove paint that has dried, use a wire brush very gently to 'unstick' the paint. Then give the brush a good rinse to remove paint flakes.

STEP 3 Don't pour paint or diluted paint into the drains. Tip it onto the grass or garden.

STEP 4 There are several ways of storing brushes, but the brush must be dry to begin with, and kept in low humidity. Wrap each brush in a thick layer of butcher's paper or newspaper.

STEP 5 Secure with string or a rubber band.

STEP 6 Either hang from a hook or place in a bucket, bristles up. Brushes can also be stored in a leather or cotton wrap.

STEP 1

STEP 2

STEP 3

PAINT ROLLERS AND TRAYS

Paint rollers are effective for painting large flat areas such as walls. There is a selection of naps available for different surfaces and textures. A short-fibre wool or acrylic roller has a general purpose nap suitable for most paints and smooth wall surfaces.

Cover the roller with plastic wrap between coats. This stops the paint drying out and saves you the work of washing and drying the roller after each coat.

It is important when cleaning a paint roller that you reduce the amount of paint on the roller to a minimum before you wash it.

STEP 1   When you've finished painting for the day, check that there's no dust or dirt in the leftover paint in the tray. If there is, discard it. If the leftover paint is clean, scrape it from the tray back into the tin.

STEP 2   Hold the roller over the paint tin. Use the paint stirrer to scrape excess paint from the roller and into the tin. Rotate the roller to make sure you scrape off all the paint.

STEP 4

STEP 3   Remove the roller from the handle. Immerse the roller in a bucket of water and continue to gently scrape the nap. When it appears that all the paint has been removed from the nap, rinse the roller in a fresh bucket of water or hose it off on the grass. Don't allow the paint to wash down the sink or drain.

STEP 4   Rinse the roller and handle. Give the roller a good shake. Towel off excess water with an old piece of towel or rag by patting, not rubbing, then allow the roller to air dry. Remove any dried paint on the handle with a wire brush or steel wool.

TIP.   Cover the paint tray with a plastic garbage bag and secure it with tape before pouring the paint into the tray. This eliminates the need to wash the tray — when you're finished, simply dispose of the plastic bag in the garbage.

SIMPLE HOUSEHOLD RECIPES

Many lotions and potions and brand names have been invented to deal with highly specific household cleaning tasks. They fill up our shopping baskets and clutter our cupboards, encouraging us to over-clean, over-deodorise and overwork.

Simplifying the type and number of products we use is better for the environment — and our own health. It takes only a small investment of time to prepare a few simple cleaning and deodorising products from materials which are inexpensive and readily available. It can save us money and make our homes more pleasant to live in.

Set aside a couple of hours every few weeks and you can produce an array of household cleaners, without the chemicals, in your own kitchen. Leftover scraps of soap or candle wax, tea still in the pot or an excess of mint from the garden can all be put to use. It's no more difficult than preparing a simple meal.

Collect interesting jars and bottles such as old preserving jars or medicine bottles to store your products in, and add scoops and spoons. The jars and bottles can make an unusual and interesting display on the laundry shelf.

Remember that any homemade recipes or formulas need to be stored correctly, labelled correctly and kept out of the reach of children.

FABRIC WASHES

Commercial washes for fabrics are often suitable for most clothing but not delicate enough for general household linens and woollens. They contain chemicals and detergents which can wear down the fibres of some fabrics and wools. Make your own fabric and wool washes that are safe for fabrics, the environment and the family. Remember that soaking can help lessen the amount of the wash required for cleaning, and it's preferable to use tepid water rather than cold or hot.

STEP 1

STEP 2

STEP 3

EUCALYPTUS WOOL WASH

This wool wash is great for sheepskin and cowhide rugs, as the oil prevents the skin from drying hard. It's also good for hand-knits and woollen blankets. It can be used in a top-loading washing machine, or for hand-washing.

6 cups pure soap flakes or grated soap
1 cup methylated spirits
2 tablespoons eucalyptus oil

STEP 1   Stir the soap and methylated spirits together in a large bowl until they are well mixed.

STEP 2   Add the eucalyptus oil and mix well. Store in a labelled jar with a wide top.

STEP 4

STEP 3   Use one tablespoon of the mixture per item. Dissolve in warm to hot water before adding to the washing water. There is no need to rinse, unless the garment is white, in which case it does need to be rinsed to prevent yellowing.

STEP 4   Squeeze the excess water from the item, roll it in a towel to remove more water, then lay flat to dry.

STEP 1

STEP 2

STEP 3

HA*nd*Y HI*n*T.

You can buy dried lavender already bunched or packaged, or dry your own. Tie the lavender into small bunches and hang in a dry, well-ventilated area. When the lavender has dried, scrape the flowers off and store in muslin or paper bags.

LAVENDER WOOL WASH

½ cup dried lavender
1 litre boiling water
2 cups pure soap flakes or grated soap
1 tablespoon bicarbonate of soda

STEP 1   Place the lavender in a bowl and pour the boiling water over it. Leave to steep several hours, or overnight.

STEP 2   Strain the liquid through muslin into a saucepan, and bring it to the boil. Discard the lavender.

STEP 3   Add the soap flakes and the bicarbonate of soda, and stir until dissolved. The mixture will turn jelly-like. Store in a sealed, labelled jar.

For machine washing, use 1 cup for a full load. If washing a blanket in a sink, use half a cup dissolved in water. Add the wool wash to the water first, then add the woollens and wash and rinse as normal.

CLEANING

A few simple recipes for cleaning will do for most surfaces. Generally a little elbow grease is the missing ingredient. A good microfibre cloth, a mop and a good quality chamois will remove grease and dirt from most surfaces, and if the surfaces are cleaned regularly to avoid any build-up of soap scum and grime, there is often no need to use chemicals. Making your own cleaning recipes is cost-effective — and a great way to use leftover tea!

VINEGAR AND DETERGENT SOLUTION

This is a good cleaning solution for the shower, the bath and ceramic tiles. If you have not had success cleaning bathrooms with vinegar in the past, it's because vinegar alone is not enough to cut through a waxy or greasy build-up. Just add a small amount of detergent to cut the grease or wax, and the vinegar will clean and disinfect. This mixture will also remove soap scum that builds up on tiles and glass. The non-abrasive formula is ideal for reconditioned cast iron baths.

Mix 1 part white vinegar to 3 parts water, and add a few drops of detergent.

TEA AND GLYCERINE SOLUTION

This solution is good for cleaning windows and glass. Use leftover black tea (strain any leaves out first) and a few drops of glycerine. Combine in a spray bottle and shake well. Spray onto the glass. Use a lint-free or microfibre cloth to clean.

EUCALYPTUS CLEANING SOLUTION

This is a gentle cleaner and disinfectant for timber or linoleum floors. It's effective whether the floors have a wax or polyurethane finish.

Add half a teaspoon of eucalyptus oil and 2 tablespoons of methylated spirits to a half-full bucket of hot water.

The mop should be wrung almost dry so no water is left to pool, allowing the floor to dry quickly. A microfibre mop is preferable, as it cleans by holding the dirt within the mop, rather than spreading it. It will also wring out drier than most other mops.

Mop the floor over, and allow to dry. There is no need to rinse the floor.

TEA AND GLYCERINE SOLUTION

T i P.   A few drops of tea tree oil on cotton wool will help remove stubborn labels, and will also remove residue left by tape or glue. Wash thoroughly with hot water and detergent to remove the tea tree oil residue, rinse under hot water, then dry.

FRESHENING UP

A naturally fresh home beats one scented by chemical deodorisers or air fresheners! Open the windows, doors and cupboards. Keep rooms well-ventilated, and allow in lots of natural sunlight. Grow scented geraniums or beautiful summer lilies outside windows. Dust and clean regularly, and use natural products for room scents. Freshly picked flowers, crushed mint or pennyroyal in a bowl, air-dried linen, chopped herbs on the kitchen bench — all will help to keep the home feeling and smelling fresh.

HANDY HINT.

Elm gum turpentine — which you can purchase from furniture restorers — is naturally aromatic and has a delightfully crisp, fresh smell. You might recognise it as one of the ingredients used in beeswax furniture polish. Dilute the turpentine with an equal amount of water and wipe down floors and furniture using a cloth dampened with the solution. Or use a couple of drops in a humidifier or spray bottle and spray through the rooms.

DEODORISING ROOM SPRAY

1 cup distilled water
2 teaspoons rubbing alcohol
3 drops lemongrass essential oil
3 drops grapefruit essential oil
3 drops orange essential oil

Combine ingredients in a spray bottle and shake well.

Adjust the nozzle to a fine or light mist setting and spray towards the ceiling, allowing the mixture to distribute itself through the air. Don't spray the mixture directly onto furniture.

EMPTY PERFUME BOTTLES MAKE GREAT CONTAINERS FOR ROOM SPRAY

LAVENDER LINEN WATER

Mix about 10 drops of lavender essential oil into 500 ml of distilled water. Use in the iron, or put into a spray bottle to spray onto linens when ironing them.

As an option, you can add to the mixture 2 drops of rose essential oil. (It need not be pure rose essential oil.)

AIR FRESHENER

Place a small dish of bicarbonate of soda in each room to absorb odours.

POTPOURRI

Rose potpourri Rose petals and a few drops of rose essential oil in a bowl or on a plate can be used to scent a room. It will smell more beautiful if the roses are scented, but scented roses are not always available. Just top up with a couple of drops of rose essential oil (3 per cent in a carrier oil) every 5 to 7 days.

The petals need to be tossed every day or so to allow them to air dry. Be careful not to jam the bowl full of petals, as the air needs to circulate around the petals to dry them—otherwise they'll turn to slush or go mouldy.

The petals won't dry if the weather is humid, but an alternative is to use petals or buds that have been dried commercially or air-dried by hanging upside-down. Place these in a bowl and add 2 to 3 drops of the rose essential oil.

SLICE THE CITRUS FRUIT THINLY SO IT WILL NOT TAKE TOO LONG TO DRY

Citrus and mint Cut citrus fruits such as orange, lemon and grapefruit into paper-thin slices, lay the slices on paper towel and leave them to air-dry in a cool room. This will generally take a few days, but it will depend on weather conditions such as humidity, and the water content of the fruit. Or dry the slices in a microwave by placing them on a paper towel and heating on a very low setting for a couple of minutes at a time. Small slices of the peel alone, without the fruit or pith (the white part under the peel), curl as they dry, and when mixed with the slices give a wonderful textural contrast.

The oils in the citrus fruits are fragrant. Toss with dried spearmint or common mint for a fresh-scented potpourri. Add a few drops of mint and citrus essential oils every 5 to 7 days to keep the scent fresh.

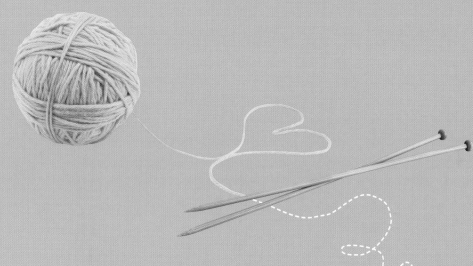

PROJECTS

SIMPLE, CRAFTY IDEAS TO GIVE YOUR HOME A LIFT

HAND STITCH

From crude, utilitarian stitching to the most delicate of silk embroidery, hand stitching is a great way to add contrast, texture, colour and pattern to projects, and can be used boldly or with subtlety.

Hand stitching requires very little equipment and can be used to create effects not achievable with a sewing machine. As well as being decorative, it has practical uses — you can use it for simple projects and repairs, for attaching appliqué and for joining heavy fabrics that a sewing machine can't manage.

Knowing just a few simple stitches such as running stitch, blanket stitch and backstitch will enable you to make beautiful items. Be creative when choosing thread and fabric. Suede, wool felt, muslin and cotton are all good backgrounds for hand stitching. Linen, embroidery thread, wool or string all make wonderful decorative stitches. However, if using hand stitching to join fabrics, be sure to take into account the strength and durability of the thread.

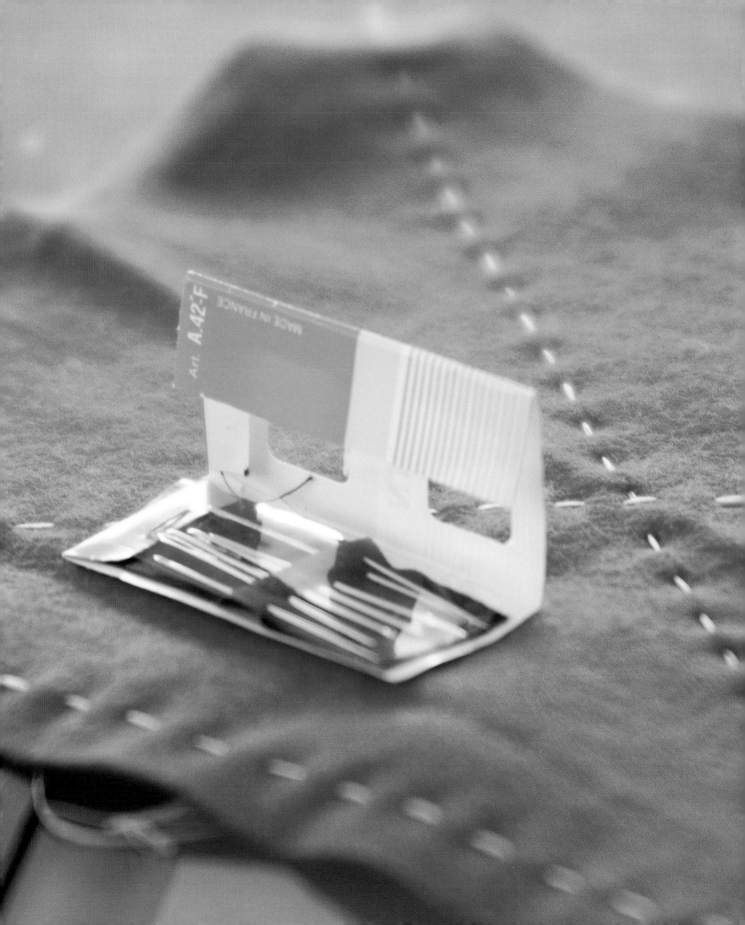

SOME SIMPLE STITCHES

When stitching, keep the tension of the thread consistent and the length of the stitches even.
Long running stitches, known as tacking or basting, can be used to join the pieces of fabric together
before you do the actual stitching. After stitching, simply snip the tacking and pull it out.

BACK STITCH

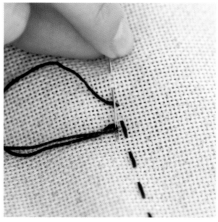

RUNNING STITCH

WHIP STITCH

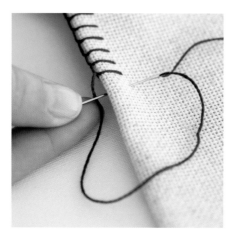

BLANKET STITCH

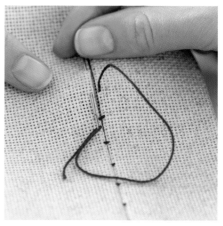

SLIP STITCH

To begin hand stitching, secure the thread with a knot on the wrong side of the work, or with a repeated backstitch.

Back stitch is a strong stitch that is very useful for sewing seams by hand. On the right side the stitches look similar to those made by a sewing machine. On the reverse side the stitches will overlap slightly.

Running stitch is used as a decorative stitch, as well as for gathering, joining and tacking.

Whip stitch can be used to join two finished edges together. Make small stitches, keeping close to the edge of the fabric and catching just a few fabric threads at a time.

Blanket stitch was traditionally used to prevent the raw edges of blankets from unravelling. However, these days it is more often used as a decorative stitch.

Slip stitch is an almost invisible way of joining two folded edges. The needle is slipped under a fold of fabric between stitches. This stitch can be used to attach trims, secure hems and to close gaps on items such as cushion covers after they have been turned right-side out.

To finish off, secure your hand stitching with a few back stitches on the spot or by looping through the threads on the wrong side of the work and tying off with a knot.

POTHOLDER BATHMAT

A thick mat made from knitted rag potholders will protect your feet from a cold bathroom floor. The mat will absorb moisture well and the uneven cotton squares give it a rustic appeal.

Because the bathmat will be exposed to moisture, the thread used to sew the squares together needs to be durable. Use linen or cotton thread, or even a lightweight cord. Avoid using string, though, as generally it's not very strong and deteriorates quite rapidly.

The potholders are inexpensive to buy already made up from kitchen or department stores, but a competent knitter can also make their own.

If you are going to knit your own rag squares, use 1 cm (⅜ in) cotton tape, or 2 cm (¾ in) cotton tape cut in half all the way along the length, or cotton poplin cut into 1 cm strips. You will need about 30 metres (33 yards) in total, but it will depend on the thickness of the material, the needle size you use and the tension of the knitting. Keep the knitting tight by using a smaller than average knitting needle — start with a needle size of approximately 5 or 6 mm (¼ in). You may need to experiment to decide what will work best for you.

The stitching will be easier if you set up your work first on a flat surface. Pin the potholders together before you start stitching, using safety pins. (Dressmaking pins won't hold the pieces together for long.)

STEP 3

STEP 4

YOU WILL NEED.

4–6 potholders or rag squares

Safety pins

Tapestry needle

Strong thread

STEP 1   Lay the pieces together in a pattern and pin them together using safety pins.

STEP 2   Do a double stitch first to secure the thread. Check that the thread is holding by giving it a little tug.

STEP 3   Now use whip stitch to stitch all the pieces together.

STEP 4   Work the needle and thread between the potholder stitches rather than forcing it through the rag.

STEP 5   Go over the stitching again. This will give you a stronger and more durable result.

STEP 6   Finish off by doing a double stitch and pushing the needle though the loop before pulling it tight, thus creating a knot.

LEATHER WRAP JOURNAL

A handmade leather cover gives a journal an appealing, informal look, as well as protecting the journal and giving it structure.

Leather is easy to work with and requires no hemming. Rawhide, suede and sheepskin can all be easily cut with scissors. For simple projects like this one there is no need for specialised tools.

Leather is available from specialty stores in many finishes, but raw leather will give this project a well-aged appearance. Raw leather is generally available in the whole hide. The grain and thickness of each hide will vary, which makes it preferable to handpick the hide. Leather shoelace is generally available from the same leather specialty stores by the metre, or from shoe repairers.

Decide what size journal you want to make. This may depend on the paper or leather you already have. The leather needs to be the height of the paper plus 4 cm (1½ in), and two-and-a-half times the width of the folded paper.

HANDY HINT.

Depending on how many pages you wish to have and the thickness of the paper you are using, you may need to fold several sections of paper inserts. Tie each section of paper separately, and ensure that the slits in the leather cover are large enough to hold the extra laces.

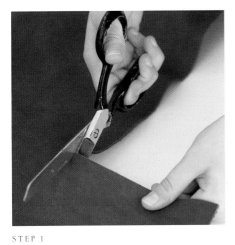

STEP 1

STEP 2

STEP 3

STEP 4

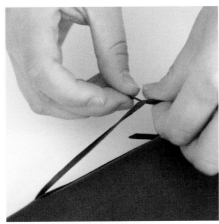

STEP 5

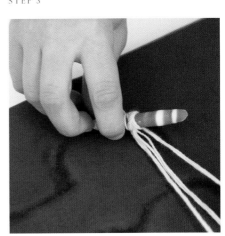

STEP 6

STEP 1   When choosing where to cut the leather, be conscious of what is on the side you will see, as you may want to make a feature of a branding mark, grain or texture. Measure the size of the journal. Add 4 cm (1½ in) to the height, and measure two-and-a-half times the width of the folded paper, and mark this onto the leather with a pencil and ruler. Use a set square to make sure the corners are square. Cut along the pencil lines using sharp scissors.

STEP 2   You will need to fold the paper in half and use the fold for the seam that holds the journal together. Place the corners of the paper together and press a fold. Open the paper up and place a steel ruler along this line. Run the back of a knife blade down this line without cutting it. Fold the paper on this line, then run the steel ruler down the edge to sharpen the fold. Repeat for the other pages.

STEP 3   Place the leather right-side-down, with the paper on top of it. Place the paper 2 cm (¾ in) from the left-hand side, so the flap for wrapping is on the right-hand side. Use a pencil to mark two holes approximately 4 cm (1½ in) apart on the fold line, for the leather shoelace to be tied through. An A5 journal will only need one set of holes, but a larger sized journal may need two sets of holes, spaced evenly. Using a sharp craft knife, cut a small slit through the paper. Then, separately, cut a slit in the leather, making sure the slits in the paper and leather align.

STEP 4   Thread the leather shoelace through the paper, then the leather. If you have trouble because the holes are tight, use the end of the fine knitting needle or crochet hook to push it through.

STEP 5   Tie the shoelace off on the outside of the journal, using a tight knot. Trim, leaving a small length on each end.

STEP 6   Cut a length of string to wrap around the journal and secure the covers, tying one end to a shell or twig.

BLANKET-STITCHED CUSHION

Here, a striking blanket-stitch border is used to transform a plain felt cushion into something more decorative. Craft felt is readily available from craft stores. It is reasonably priced and has the advantage that it does not fray. If you want to add a special touch, you could use handmade wool felt.

STEP 1

STEP 2

STEP 3

YOU WiLL Need.

Cushion insert

Felt

Fabric marker or pencil that fades

Ruler

Sewing machine (optional)

Thread the same colour as the felt

Pins

Embroidery thread, silk thread or wool (a contrasting colour is ideal for the decorative stitch)

Suitable needle for your chosen thread

STEP 1   Measure and mark two felt squares to fit your cushion insert and cut them out. The squares should be the size of the cushion insert plus 10 mm (½ in) on all sides (e.g. for a 45 cm x 45 cm cushion insert you will need to cut two squares of felt 47 cm x 47 cm).

STEP 2   Pin the seams on the felt 10 mm (½ in) from the edge. Pin all four sides, leaving a 15 cm (6 in) gap on the last side. It doesn't matter whether the gap is in the middle or on the side. The cushion will be inserted through this gap and the gap closed with hand stitching.

STEP 3   Using a medium length stitch, machine stitch the seams, reversing a couple of stitches at the beginning and end to prevent the stitching from unravelling. Insert the cushion through the gap. Pin and tack the gap, then close it using backstitch. It is essential to pin and tack first so that the hand stitching follows a straight line. The seams will act as a guide to keep the blanket stitching perfectly even in length.

STEP 4   Blanket stitch the edge of the pillow. Try to keep the stitches as even as possible. This can be achieved by drawing lines first, using a fabric pencil or marker pen that fades. At each corner, work a diagonal stitch.

FELT ROSETTE CUSHIONS

A plain white linen cushion cover can be given a striking makeover using rosettes made from layers of felt in contrasting colours. Or instead of using contrasting colours, you could also try white on white for a textural cushion.

Felt does not fray, which means that no hemming is required. This makes it a very easy fabric to work with.

A pleasing pattern is achieved through the repetition of colours and circles. The rosette is made using a simple stitch that gathers at the back.

STEP 1

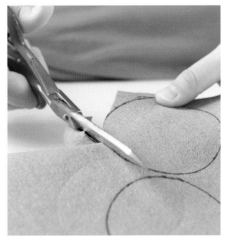

STEP 2

STEP 3

STEP 1   Place the circular template on the felt and use a felt-tip pen to draw an outline of the circle. Mark the circle gently to avoid dragging or warping the felt. (Fabric pencils or tailor's chalk are not appropriate for felt, as they drag the fibres.) You will need 25 circles. Keep the circles close together so that there is less waste. Repeat for all three colours of felt, using a different size template for each colour.

STEP 2   Carefully cut out all the circles using sharp dressmaking scissors.

STEP 3   Layer the circles, largest to smallest, making sure any pen outline is not on the facing side. Place the largest circle right side up, place the next size circle in the centre also right side up, and then lastly the smallest circle, also centred.

YOU will need.

Wool felt in three colours

Three circular templates measuring 2 cm (¾ in), 4 cm (1½ in) and 6 cm (2½ in) — use tins, jars or even coins in the desired size

Felt-tip pen or fabric marker

Dressmaking scissors

Pins

Needle and thread

40 cm x 40 cm (16 in x 16 in) cushions with removable covers

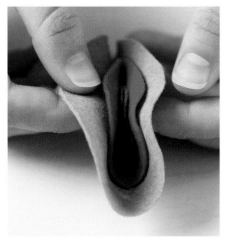

STEP 4

STEP 5

STEP 6

STEP 7

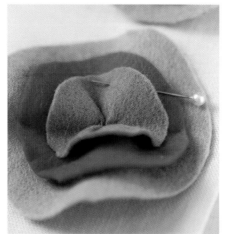

STEP 8

STEP 9

STEP 4   Fold all the layers in half, with the right sides together.

STEP 5   To gather the felt, make a stitch through all three layers of the felt about 5 mm (¼ in) in from the fold. Repeat several times, passing the needle through the same place each time. Pull the stitches tight. Finish by looping the thread through the back layers of the stitching several times and pulling tightly. This will help with the gathering of the rosette. Tie off firmly.

STEP 6   Unfold, then refold the circles at right angles to the previous fold. As you have a gathered stitch already, the circles will not sit flat.

STEP 7   Place several strong stitches 5 mm (¼ in) from the fold, as before, so that there is a cross in the centre. Finish as before by looping the thread through the back layers of the stitching several times and pulling tightly. Tie off firmly. You should now have a rosette. Repeat for the other 24.

STEP 8   Pin five rows of five rosettes to the cushion cover.

STEP 9   Stitch through all layers of the rosette onto the cover using five or six strong stitches.

HANDKERCHIEF PINCUSHION

Although handkerchiefs are not widely used anymore, many beautiful handkerchiefs are still to be found in fine linen stores or at second-hand markets. Here's a practical and beautiful idea for making a handkerchief into a pincushion. The handkerchief need not be cut, but can simply be folded in such a way that it can be stitched around the polyester wadding.

STEP 1

STEP 2

STEP 3

STEP 4

YOU will need.

Linen or cotton handkerchief

Polyester wadding (available from craft stores) folded into four or six layers, or a piece of foam 10 cm x 14 cm (4 in x 5½ in)

Pins

Fine needle and thread

STEP 1   Wash the handkerchief first, using a natural soap. Rinse well, adding a couple of drops of lavender oil to the rinse water. Hang out to dry, then iron flat — you may need to dampen down the linen first.

Place the handkerchief right side down and fold into thirds. The folded width of the handkerchief needs to be 5 mm (¼ in) wider than the wadding. You may need to adjust the fold on the handkerchief to fit.

STEP 2   Place the wadding on top of the hanky and loosely roll the wadding and handkerchief together. Tuck in any loose ends.

STEP 3   Pin the seams of the handkerchief together at both ends and at the front.

STEP 4   Whip stitch the sides and front of the handkerchief, using delicate stitches. Be careful not to stitch into the wadding.

PILLOW COVER

You can keep a fresh, updated look in the bedroom by changing the soft furnishings or bed linen. Bedroom coordinates are expensive, but instead of purchasing a whole new set of linen, add your own stitched designs, like these easy spirals, for colour and texture. The designs could be used on a doona cover, pillows, cushions, cotton blankets, even a simple bedside lamp, to transform the room.

If working within a budget, buy solid coloured linen as separates — it's often cheaper. Buy good quality cotton bed linen where the budget allows and use cotton thread, as it gives a better result.

YOU will need.

Tracing paper, lunch wrap or greaseproof paper

Pencil or pen

Pins

Scissors

Cotton or silk embroidery threads (One skein of cotton thread of each colour will be enough for several pillows in a simple design.)

Pillow covers

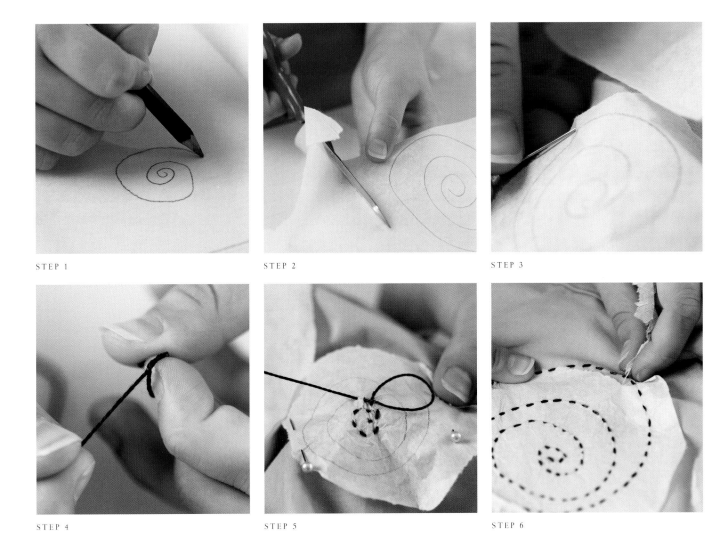

STEP 1

STEP 2

STEP 3

STEP 4

STEP 5

STEP 6

STEP 1   Draw the spirals freehand onto the paper using pencil or pen, keeping your wrist loose and your hand relaxed. Keep them fairly loose, especially in the centre. If the spiral is too tight at the centre, you may not be able to stitch the circular turns neatly. Don't allow the loops of the spiral to touch, as this will make it difficult to stitch. If you are stitching several spirals, make them in varying sizes so the composition is less structured.

STEP 2   Once you are happy with the spirals, roughly cut around the design, leaving enough extra paper to pin it to the fabric. Place several spirals onto the pillow cover to decide on final design placement.

STEP 3   Pin the design onto the pillow cover. You will be stitching straight through the paper and the fabric at the same time.

STEP 4   To hold the thread in place, tie a small knot at the end of the thread and pass the thread through the centre of the spiral from the wrong side. (Securing the thread with back stitching or a double knot will look too heavy.)

STEP 5   Using running stitch, stitch on the design, starting from the middle of the spiral. To finish off, secure the thread on the reverse side by double stitching under another stitch and tying a knot. Trim the thread.

STEP 6   Very gently tear off the paper. If necessary, hold the stitching in place with a fingertip while you do this. Press the finished pillow cover with a hot iron from the wrong side.

BLANKET-STITCHED SHAWL CUSHION

Perhaps you have a shawl or scarf at the bottom of the drawer that was a 'must have' several years ago, but which you no longer feel the same way about. A shawl is generally lighter than a wool blanket and often uses a soft mix of cashmere with lambswool. This makes it ideal as a cover for a soft, loose pillow that you can toss onto the lounge and snuggle up to on a rainy Sunday.

As the woven edges (the selvedge) of the shawl need no hemming, they can simply be sewn up with a decorative blanket stitch in the same colour thread, or in a contrasting colour. This is a slip cover, so an opening is left through which you can slip the cushion into the cover, and there is no fastening. The end of the shawl overlaps the opening, and the shawl's fringe provides a decorative edging.

STEP 1

STEP 2

STEP 3

YOU will need.

Rectangular shawl or scarf

Cushion just short of the width of the shawl or scarf

Sewing machine

Quilter's pins

Decorative thread and tapestry needle

Tacking thread and needle

STEP 1   Lay out the shawl right side down. Position the cushion so that when you fold one fringed end over it, it finishes at one-third the depth of the cushion. Fold the other end of the shawl over the top, and trim it off so that it ends 2 cm (¾ in) beyond the edge of the cushion. Remove the cushion from the shawl. Fold the cut edge of the shawl down 1 cm (⅜ in), then another 1 cm (⅜ in), and hem using the sewing machine.

STEP 2   Lay the cushion back on the shawl. Fold the hemmed edge over so that it just wraps round the cushion. Pin the sides of the shawl together using quilter's pins.

STEP 3   Blanket stitch the side seams. You can do this while the cushion is still in the cover, but if you find this awkward and would prefer to take the cushion out before you sew up the side seams, tack the seams before you remove the cushion. The cushion may be a little fiddly to get out of and back into the cover, but the tacking will hold the cover together. Take care to keep the hand stitching even.

TABLE RUNNER

Liven up a table and protect its surface at the same time by buying a simple table runner in a solid colour and adding your own touch to it. Most fabric and craft stores will have felt in a range of colours, and you may be able to purchase it pre-cut as craft squares. The stitches are decorative, so the choice of thread is important. Fine strings or ribbons, wool and metallic thread look great, but when the needle is threaded the thickness of the thread is doubled, so test thicker thread by trying out a few stitches first. This is a very simple project, suitable for beginners.

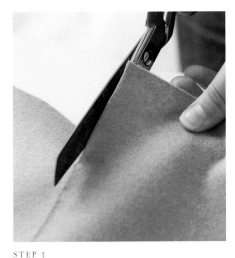

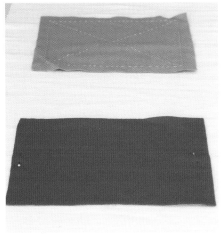

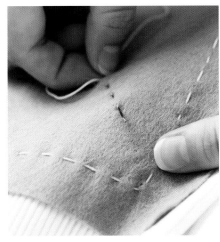

STEP 1

STEP 2

STEP 3

STEP 1   Use a fabric marker or tailor's chalk to mark a rectangle 20 cm x 30 cm (8 in x 12 in) onto each of the three colours of felt. (You can choose a larger or smaller size to suit the table runner.) Make sure that the corners are square. Be careful not to drag the felt while marking it, as this can cause it to warp.

STEP 2   Cut out the rectangles using sharp scissors. Use long cuts, following the marked lines. Place one rectangle onto the centre of the table runner, then arrange the other two evenly on each side so that the felt pieces are 10–20 cm (4–8 in) apart. Use a tape measure or ruler to make sure the distances between the felt rectangles are equal. The exact spacing will depend on the length of the table and the look you prefer. Pin the felt rectangles in place.

STEP 3   Stitch the rectangles onto the table runner using a simple running stitch. First thread the needle, then knot the thread at the longer end. Push the needle through from the back and commence the running stitch. The knot will hold the thread in place. Using a knot instead of a double stitch will prevent an extra stitch from showing. To finish off without using an obvious double stitch, take the thread through to the back and do a double stitch that doesn't go all the way through to the front side of the felt. Cut off any long threads. Once you have stitched around the edges of the rectangles, add lines of stitching across the diagonals. Finish off as before.

YOU will need.

Felt in three colours

Fabric marker or tailor's chalk

Tape measure

Scissors

Table runner in a solid colour

Pins

Needle and decorative thread

COVERED COAT-HANGER

You don't need a sewing machine to make a pretty, covered coat-hanger that you won't want to hide in the wardrobe. Slip a gorgeous garment onto it, and hang it from a door hook or handle instead. Once you have completed one and discover how simple this project is, you will want to fill your wardrobe with more coat-hangers covered in all types of beautiful fabrics.

Coat-hangers made from timber with screw-in metal hangers are readily available. Padding around the timber of the hanger will provide protection for delicate garments. Quilter's wool or cotton wadding works well and is available from quilter's stores or large fabric retailers. It's more durable than foam, which tends to break down and tear easily. Rather than sewing or gluing the wadding to the timber, an easy method is to bind it on with thread.

The cover can be made from fabric left over from other projects — it's a great way to use up small amounts of left-over fabric. Almost any cotton will work, as long as it is not too heavy. The cotton fabrics used for quilt making are ideal. Add a pretty ribbon to cover the metal hanger, and your project is complete!

YOU will need.

Wooden coat-hanger

Wool or cotton wadding

Scissors

Pins

Round template such as a jam jar lid

Thread and needle

Extra thread for binding

A piece of pretty cotton fabric at least 14 cm (5½ in) wide and twice the length of the coat-hanger plus 3 cm (1¼ in)

30 cm (12 in) length of ribbon about 6 mm (¼ in) wide

STEP 1

STEP 2

STEP 1   Unscrew the metal hook from the wooden part of the coat-hanger. Cut the cotton wadding 7 cm (2¾ in) wide by the length of the coat-hanger plus 1.5 cm (⅝ in) added to each end. To reduce the bulk when folding, cut out 90° corners at the ends.

STEP 2   Wrap the wadding tightly around the coat-hanger, turning the ends under.

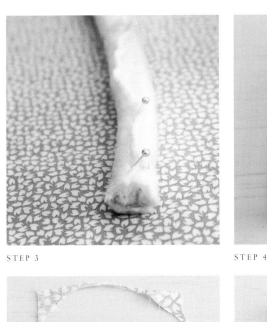

STEP 3

STEP 4

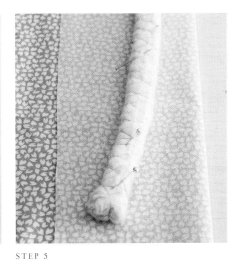

STEP 5

STEP 6

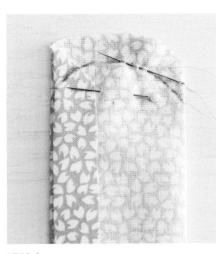

STEP 7

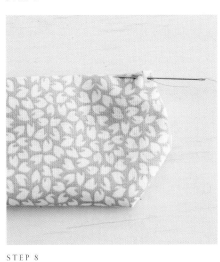

STEP 8

STEP 3   Fix the wadding tightly in place with pins.

STEP 4   Using a cotton thread, bind the wadding. Go up and back on the hanger to ensure it is wrapped up tightly. Finish off with a couple of tight knots.

STEP 5   To measure your piece of fabric, lay it flat, right side up. Fold it lengthwise so that you can measure 7 cm (2¾ in) wide. (The fabric will be 14 cm (5½ in) wide once cut and unfolded.)

The length of fabric needs to be twice that of the coat-hanger, plus a 1.5 cm (⅝ in) seam allowance at each end. So for a 40 cm (16 in) hanger, the folded fabric should measure 7 cm (2¾ in) wide by 83 cm (33 in) long. Cut the fabric.

STEP 6   Round off the corners by using the lid of a jam jar or a small upturned cup as a template. Add a 1 cm (⅜ in) seam allowance, and cut out following the rounded edge.

STEP 7   Turn 1.5 cm (⅝ in) down along the cut edge on both sides and iron flat. With the fabric still with right sides together, take a needle and thread and use tiny running stitches to stitch the seam around the rounded ends until the stitching reaches the top. Use a back stitch to secure the thread. Repeat for the other end.

STEP 8   Turn the fabric right side out and pin along the top. Using a small running stitch, sew the top pieces together. Leave a small gap of 3–4 cm (1¼–1½ in) approximately three-quarters of the way along the length to insert the coat-hanger.

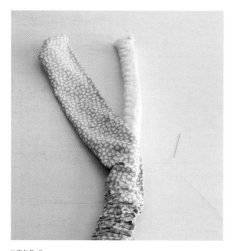

STEP 9

STEP 10

STEP 11

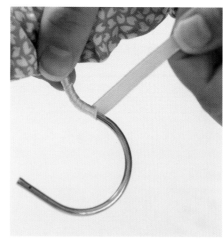

STEP 12

STEP 13

STEP 9   Insert the hanger, gently pushing the fabric along as you go. Then sew up the remaining gap with small running stitches.

STEP 10   To stop the cover from slipping, sew a couple of discreet stitches through to the wadding at each end to hold in place.

STEP 11   To work out where the hole to screw in the hook is, place the covered hanger next to another hanger with its hook removed. The visible hole in the uncovered hanger will act as a

guide. Push the end of the metal hook in between the running stitches, taking care not to break any threads. Gently move the hook about until you find the hole, then screw it in.

STEP 12   Fasten the ribbon to the cover at the base of the hook, using a small stitch.

STEP 13   Wrap the ribbon around the metal hanger. When you reach the top, trim the ribbon, leaving a small end to tuck under. Tuck under and secure to the rest of the ribbon by sewing a small stitch.

EMBELLISH

Embellishing is a wonderful way to add frivolity, colour or pattern. It can be as simple as attaching a gorgeous ribbon or beads, or as extravagant as creating a whole fantasy room.

Embellishment is often used just for fun, as decoration. But apart from adding visual interest, embellishment has some practical value as a cover-up for flaws or imperfections. A tear on a tablecloth can be hidden under a small appliquéd motif; a ribbon or a painted stencil can be used to hide a small stain.

Embellishments can be attached by stitching, gluing, machine sewing, wiring and tying. When choosing how you will attach an embellishment, take into account the purpose of the project and how it will be treated. Does it need to be able to go in the wash? Will it be kept outdoors?

Sew a ribbon onto a bed sheet or a beaded placemat to a cushion cover. Embellish with ribbons, shells, buttons, silk flowers, fringing and beading. Create distinct or random patterns. Add one beautiful glass bead, or go over the top and cram in as many bright adornments as you can. When it comes to embellishing, the only rule is to use your imagination!

KEY TASSEL

Tassels made from fine silk threads elegantly knotted and twisted are often used to add a luxurious touch to drapery and furnishings — with a price to match! Simple key tassels made from interestingly textured threads are as easy to make as a pompom and require no great skill. A decorative tassel makes a key easier to identify and less likely to be lost. The following instructions are for a medium-sized tassel. The size of the tassel can be varied by using a smaller or larger piece of cardboard.

YOU WILL NEED.

Stiff cardboard

Ball of thread

Craft scissors

Key

HANDY HINT.

Knitting stores stock unusual threads in many colours, and in textures varying from ribbon-like to feathery or metallic. Two or more colours or textures could be wound on together, or a separate colour wound around the top of the tassel.

STEP 1

STEP 2

STEP 3

STEP 4

STEP 5

STEP 6

STEP 1   Cut a piece of cardboard measuring 10 cm x 6 cm (4 in x 2¼ in). Wind the thread onto the cardboard as when making a pompom. Start the thread at one edge with 1 cm (⅜ in) overhanging. Wind the thread on as straight as possible, keeping the tension even.

STEP 2   To judge how much thread to wind onto the tassel, measure visually, and by touch. To prevent the last strand being shorter than the others, cut the strand 1 or 2 cm (⅜ or ¾ in) longer than the cardboard. This will be trimmed later.

STEP 3   Cut a 10 cm (4 in) length of thread. Take the end of the thread in between the cardboard and wrapped thread and knot the ends together. Tuck the knot out of sight behind the threads. This will be used to attach the tassel to the key.

STEP 4   Gently slide the cardboard out, holding the threads firmly so they don't move around. Take another length of thread and wrap it around the top of the tassel approximately 1.5 cm (⅝ in) from the top. Wrap firmly, keeping the tension tight. Use enough thread to give a little bulk at the top, and tie off with a knot.

STEP 5   Hold the tassel at the top and place the scissors through the loops at the bottom. You will need to put a little tension into this, to straighten out any kinked threads. Cut through the threads. Hold the tassel at the top and give it a good shake to assist the threads to fall into place. Use scissors to cut any long threads, to make the tassel even at the bottom.

STEP 6   Loop the tassel through the end of the key.

BEADED PLACEMAT CUSHION COVER

A beaded placemat has been used to decorate this cushion cover. The placemat is held in place with hand stitching, and can be removed if you need to clean the cushion cover. Stitching the placemat onto the cushion cover is easy, and takes very little time.

Look for placemats with interesting textures — woven, embroidered or beaded, or made from unusual materials such as seagrass, rushes or other natural fibres. It will make the project easier if you choose a mat that can be easily stitched to the cushion cover.

Choose a mat that is the right size to fit a cushion cover. A cot pillow is the ideal size for a placemat cushion cover. Alternatively, you could centre a smaller placemat on a large cushion, leaving a border around the placemat.

Begin by making your own cushion cover in a size and fabric of your choice. The following steps are for a finished cushion cover that measures 34 cm by 44 cm (13 in x 17 in). The cushion has an opening at the back with fastenings, or you could use buttons and buttonholes.

YOU will need.

- Cushion or small pillow insert
- Measuring tape or ruler
- Fabric to make cushion cover
- Fabric marker or tailor's chalk
- Scissors
- Dressmaking pins
- Iron
- Sewing machine
- Thread in contrasting colour for tacking
- 3 fastenings or buttons
- Placemat
- Needle and thread

STEP 1

STEP 2

STEP 1   For the front of the cushion, measure 34 cm x 44 cm (13 in x 17 in), then add 1.5 cm (⅝ in) on each side for the seam allowance.

STEP 2   Use a fabric marker or tailor's chalk to mark the fabric.

STEP 3

STEP 4

STEP 5

STEP 6

STEP 7

STEP 8

STEP 3   Cut fabric to size.

STEP 4   The back has a fastening or button opening for which you will need to make allowances. To make the two sides that overlap and fasten, divide the 44 cm (17 in) in half and add 4 cm (1½ in), giving you a measurement of 26 cm x 34 cm (10 in x 13 in). You will need two of these to make the back of the cushion cover.

STEP 5   On the edge where the cover fastens, turn under 1 cm (⅜ in), then turn under another 3 cm (1¼ in). Pin in place, using dressmaking pins.

STEP 6   Iron the flap flat.

STEP 7   Machine stitch 2 mm (¹⁄₁₆ in) from the edge to hold the hem in place. Do this to the second piece as well.

STEP 8   Pin the two parts of the back in place, one edge over the top of the other. (If you are using buttons to fasten the back cover opening, mark where the buttons and buttonholes will be placed. Referring to the sewing machine instructions, complete the buttonholes.) Pin the two back pieces to the front. Back and front pieces need to be right side together.

STEP 9

STEP 10

STEP 11

S T E P   9   Tack seams along the 1.5 cm (⅝ in) seam allowance and machine stitch on all four sides.

S T E P   1 0   Snip corners to reduce the bulk when the cushion cover is folded right side out. Add fastenings or buttons to the back opening of the cushion.

S T E P   1 1   Turn the cushion cover right side out. Stitch the placemat in place. You may need to pin or tack the placemat first, depending on the material. (The beaded placemat was tacked to the cushion cover, then hand stitched with whip stitch.)

HANdy HiNt.

Unusual and attractive placemats can be found in Asian specialty stores and in department stores. Try using natural grass, reed and coir placemats — these can be easily replaced as they wear. A rustic embellishment like this makes a cushion ideal for outdoor use, but unless the materials are designed to withstand the elements, store the cushions undercover or indoors. Even faux fur can be added to a cushion cover — cut into the shapes you require and stitch or glue it on.

You could also use plain placemats with decorative stitching added. Knitting wool, embroidery thread and kitchen string can be used, providing you are not using them on delicate fabrics. Rows of running stitches in contrasting threads make a simple and attractive embellishment.

If you want to save time, use ready-made cushion covers instead of making your own, and simply add interesting embellishments.

FLOWERED FOOD COVER

Picnics and outdoor dining are a great way to enjoy the warmer months. Food covers adorned with silk flowers and beads add frivolity and keep falling leaves and insects off the food.

Food covers are inexpensive, and easy to decorate with brightly coloured materials. Avoid using heavy objects to embellish this project, as the netting will tear, leaving holes for the bugs to get in through. Silk flower petals and lightweight beads are ideal.

YOU WILL NEED.

Food cover (purchased)

Silk flowers

Lightweight beads

Pins

Needle and thread

Scissors

STEP 1

STEP 2

STEP 3

STEP 4

STEP 5

STEP 1   Decide where to put the beads and flowers. Pinning the flowers onto the cover first may help you visualise what it will look like. If the food cover is the kind that closes, check that the design won't get caught up in the umbrella folds.

STEP 2   Tie a knot at the end of the thread to hold the first stitch in place. Bring the needle from the inside of the food cover through to hold a flower in place. Put a couple of stitches through the flower.

STEP 3   Add a bead by sliding the needle through the bead hole, then back through the flower.

STEP 4   Make sure the thread holds the bead in place, but don't pull it too tight. Finish by doing a couple of double stitches at the back.

STEP 5   If the cover has a string, add a final flourish with a few beads, making sure that the cover will still open and close.

TIP.   Carry your food cover design over to a simple jug or bowl cover. If you don't have a ready-made cover, use tulle or muslin. Cut a circle of the fabric that is approximately 10 cm (4 in) larger in diameter than the opening of the jug. Hand stitch a small rolled hem using using whip stitch or slipstitch. Add strings of beads to the hem, spaced out evenly around it. The weight of the beads will hold the cover in place. Use the same flowers and beads you used for the food cover to decorate the jug cover.

SEW

A sewing machine can be a great asset in brightening up your home. You only need a few basic skills to be able to pull out the machine and whip up new cushion covers, curtains, throws, pillow covers, placemats and table runners.

There are different sewing machines for different levels of capability and budgets. If you only intend sewing simple soft furnishings made from ordinary fabrics, you may only require a basic sewing machine. If you intend to sew heavy canvas or leather regularly, you might consider an industrial or semi-industrial machine. For dressmaking, you could consider buying an overlocker as well.

Shop around for a sewing machine, and if you are a beginner consider taking the few lessons that most suppliers offer. Learning those few basics will make all the difference to the projects you are able to tackle.

Shop for fabrics and threads through discount fabric houses or at sales so you have materials on hand when inspiration strikes. From simple fresh cottons to exotic silks or cashmere, there is an endless array of beautiful fabrics to choose from.

It's a great feeling to be able to reinvent a room with a change of cushion covers or curtains and a new throw — and it takes very little time and money.

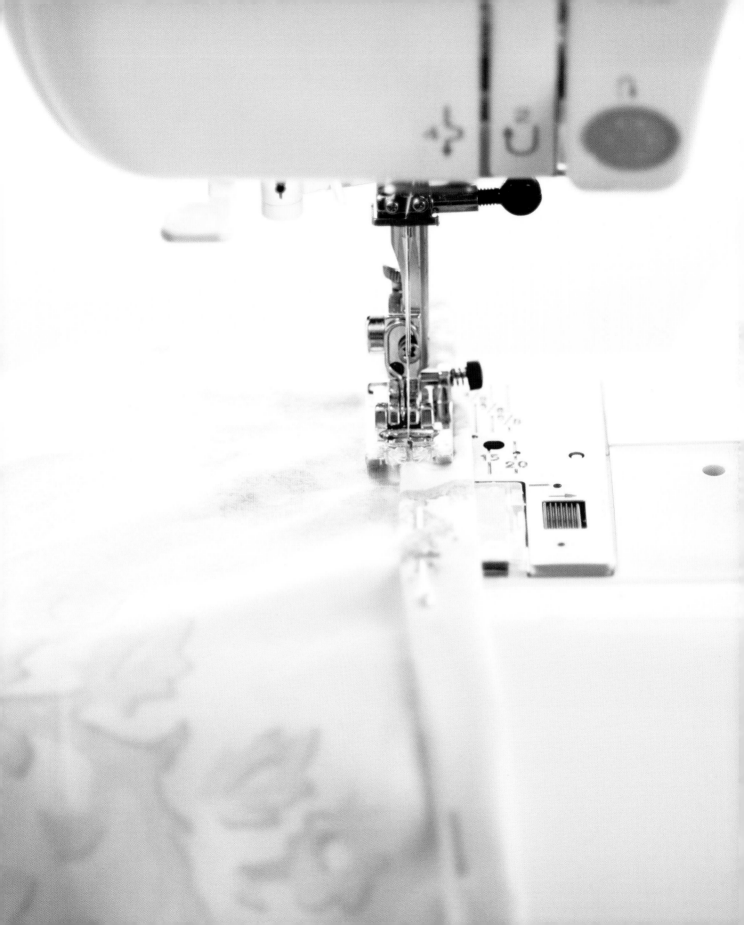

MOHAIR-BLANKET PILLOWS

YOU will need.

Mohair blanket

Pillow

Ruler

Tailor's chalk

Dressmaking scissors

Quilter's pins

Sewing machine

Thread to match the blanket

Three fasteners such as large press-studs

Keeping warm in winter is as much about surrounding yourself with warm colours, textures and lighting as it is about rugging up in warm clothing. These mohair-covered pillows will have you feeling as cosy as can be.

Any mohair blanket can be used for this project, whether it be an old travel rug, unused blankets you have sitting in the cupboard, or a cot blanket that's a bit threadbare in patches.

If there is a fringe on the blanket, consider whether you will use it to fringe the pillow. Take into account any patterns or areas that you want to include, and note whether there are checks or stripes to match up.

If you are unsure where to cut the blanket, lay a tracing paper template (include seam allowances) onto the blanket to help you to work out the design.

STEP 1

STEP 2

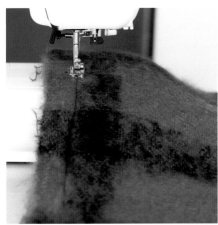

STEP 3

STEP 4

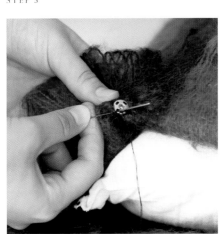

STEP 5

STEP 6

S T E P 1   Measure the size of the pillow you wish to cover. Add a 2 cm (¾ in) seam allowance on three sides. At the opening end, add 12 cm (4¾ in) — this is 2 cm (¾ in) for the seam allowance and 10 cm (4 in) for the opening. If you are using a raw edge, add another 2 cm (¾ in) to allow for a turned hem. Draw the measurements on using tailor's chalk. (Fabric pencils and markers will not work well on mohair.)

S T E P 2   Cut along the lines, and pin the two pieces together on three sides with right sides facing on three seams. Use long quilting pins with coloured heads so the pins don't get lost in the mohair.

S T E P 3   Leave a 2 cm (¾ in) seam allowance and machine stitch three sides. When feeding the blanket under the foot and needle of the sewing machine, try to keep the fibres flat, otherwise they will become tangled on top of the foot. If you are not using

fringing or a selvedge at the opening, you will need to hem the fourth side. Turn the edge under 1 cm (⅜ in) then turn under again. Hand-stitch the hem using slip stitch to give a neat finish.

S T E P 4   Trim the bulk of the blanket off the corners by cutting across them diagonally. Be sure to cut a few millimetres away from the seam, to avoid snipping into it.

S T E P 5   Turn the cover right side out. Place the pillow inside the cover to measure where to place the fastenings. You will need at least two or three fastenings across the opening. Mark where each one goes using a pin or a stitch.

S T E P 6   Hand stitch the fastenings onto the inside of the cover. If you wish, you can sew decorative buttons onto the outside, in the same positions. These will prevent any stitches from the press-studs showing on the front side of the cover.

SIMPLE PILLOW COVER

YOU *will* N*eed*.

2 m (78 in) of fabric

Scissors

Dressmaking pins

Thread to match fabric

Sewing machine

Iron

Although fabric can be expensive, it's possible to find small lengths as remnants at bargain prices. It may be the end of a roll, or just one or two metres, but that is enough to make cushion covers or napkins, or to cover a box.

You only need about 2 metres (2 yards) of fabric to make a cover for a standard bedroom pillow of 50 cm x 66 cm (20 in x 26 in). Depending on the width of the fabric, you may be able to get two pillow covers from it.

Some fabrics shrink when they are washed for the first time, so you should wash and dry the fabric before cutting and sewing. Iron the fabric flat before you begin to measure, so that the pattern is exact.

STEP 1

STEP 2

STEP 3

STEP 1   Fold the fabric in half. You want the fold on the opposite end to the opening for the pillow. Measure 86.5 cm (34 in) in length and 53 cm (20 in) wide. Use the selvedge for one of the long sides. When you unfold the fabric, you will have one piece measuring 53 cm (20 in) wide by 173 cm (68 in) long. To hem the short ends, turn under 5 mm (3/16 in), wrong sides together, then another 1 cm (3/8 in) to create a double fold. Pin the folds.

STEP 2   Iron the hem flat. Repeat for the other end. Sew both hems using the sewing machine.

STEP 3   With right sides together, fold the fabric so that one side measures 76 cm (30 in) and the other side measures 94 cm (37 in). Place the fabric on a flat surface such as a bench or table, with the longer side underneath. The bottom side should be 18 cm (7 in) longer than the top side. Pin the sides.

STEP 4   Fold the 18 cm (7 in) flap over the top, making sure the fold lines up exactly with the end of the side seam. This will appear to close off the opening, but it will reappear when the pillow cover is turned right way out. Now, sew up the side seams and turn the pillow cover right way out. Iron and insert a pillow.

SACK PILLOWS

Sack pillows are a novel way to decorate a toddler's bedroom. Children love to drag things around behind them, and the pillow is perfect, as it's soft and lightweight.

The sack needs to be larger than the pillow, as it is meant to be oversized and floppy. Use bright colours and natural fabrics such as cotton and flannelette. The fabrics need to be fairly durable as toddlers' pillow covers seem to spend more time in the wash than they do on the bed.

YOU WILL NEED.

Two pieces of fabric, each measuring 103 cm x 58 cm (40 in x 23 in)

Scissors

Pins

Tacking thread

Iron

Sewing machine

Matching thread

Pillow 50 cm x 66 cm (20 in x 26 in)

Cord or ribbon

HANDY HINT.

If you are pinning a straight seam, place the pin across the seam rather than pinning lengthways. This will enable you to sew over the pins. Be careful, though, that the sewing machine needle doesn't hit a pin. If it does, the needle is likely to break. This technique takes a little practice, but will save time.

STEP 1

STEP 2

STEP 3

STEP 4

STEP 5

STEP 6

S T E P   1   Cut the fabric pieces to size.

S T E P   2   Place the fabric pieces with the right sides together and pin three seams, leaving the top open. If the fabric has a pattern, make sure both pieces are right way up.

S T E P   3   Tack then machine sew the three seams. As it's a straightforward seam, you don't need to tack if you feel confident that you can sew with the pins still in place.

S T E P   4   Still with right sides facing inside, turn the top down 1 cm (⅜ in), then another 1 cm (⅜ in), giving the top opening a double fold. Tack and iron flat.

S T E P   5   Machine stitch the hem of the rolled top. Remove the tacking stitches.

S T E P   6   Insert the pillow and tie the cord tightly.

T I P.   When cutting out fabric, make use of the selvedge and use this as a 'cut' edge. It will save sewing raw edges and give a neater finish. Use a set square, square to the selvedge, to get perfect 90 degree corners.

TEA TOWEL TABLE RUNNER

The humble tea towel, with its durable fabric and simple designs, is perfect for creating cushion covers and napkins. Two or more tea towels can even be joined together to make a casual table runner. This simple idea makes a great project for a beginner new to the sewing machine.

YOU WiLL Need.

Two or more linen or cotton tea towels in the same design

Seam ripper or unpicker

Iron

Pins

Sewing machine

Matching thread

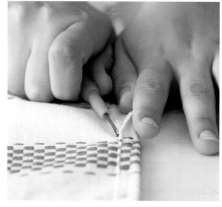
STEP 1

STEP 2

STEP 3

STEP 4

STEP 5

STEP 1   Unpick the hem at one end of the tea towel with a seam ripper, taking care not to cut the tea towel. Unless there are selvedges at the side, you will also need to unpick a few centimetres of both the side hems, starting from the end with the unpicked hem. Repeat for the other tea towel.

STEP 2   Use a hot iron to iron the unpicked hem flat.

STEP 3   Place the tea towels together with right sides facing each other and pin together. Make sure the pattern lines up.

STEP 4   Using a straight stitch, machine sew the two tea towels together. Use a couple of reverse stitches at the start and the end. To stop the raw edges from unravelling, you will need to overlock or zigzag them. Overlock or zigzag each edge separately.

STEP 5   Iron the seam flat. Fold the side seams that were unpicked to match the rest of the seam, and press with a hot iron. Pin them, then machine stitch them in place. Repeat steps 1 to 5 if adding another tea towel. Iron the finished table runner.

BERIBBONED TABLE RUNNER

As an informal alternative to a tablecloth, a table runner is decorative as well as giving some protection to the table. Table runners are ideal for casual or outdoor dining, and can be combined with matching placemats and napkins.

Table runners usually run the length of the table and they may run over the ends of the table — there are no hard and fast rules as to where they should finish. You can vary the length of the runner to suit the length of the table, and your own taste.

YOU WILL NEED.

Cotton or linen fabric measuring 63 cm (25 in) wide by the length required for your table (including extra for seam allowances)

Dressmaking pins

Tape measure

Fabric pen

Scissors

Matching thread

Ribbon

Needle and thread for tacking

Sewing machine

Iron

HANDY HINT.

Natural linens or cottons are practical choices of fabric because they are machine washable. Check that any ribbons or embellishments you use are machine washable and colour fast as well.

STEP 1

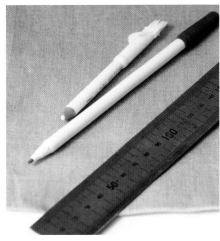

STEP 2

STEP 3

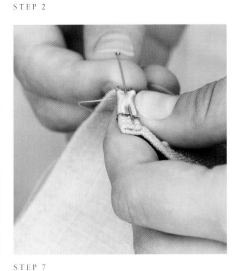

STEP 6

STEP 7

STEP 8

STEP 1   Select your fabric and a ribbon that complements it.

STEP 2   Measure the length required for your table runner. You will need to allow an extra 1.5 cm (⅝ in) for the seam at each end. Lay the fabric flat. Using a selvedge side, measure 63 cm (25 in). Mark with a fabric pencil, then cut to size.

STEP 3   To hem the table runner, make a 5 mm (³⁄₁₆ in) fold on one side, then fold under again, this time 1 cm (⅜ in), tucking the raw edges under. Pin in place.

STEP 4   Do this for the other three sides. Press flat with a hot iron.

STEP 5   Machine stitch around the table runner's hem, turning at the corners and finishing with a couple of back stitches.

STEP 6   Pin the ribbon in place.

STEP 7   Turn the end of the ribbon under the edge of the table runner and pin this in place.

STEP 8   Machine stitch the ribbon onto the runner, removing the pins as you sew. If you don't feel confident doing this, tack the ribbon in place before sewing. This will hold it exactly in position and help give an even tension. Remove the tacking stitches once the machine stitching is done.

KNIT

Knitting swings in and out of fashion as new yarns and patterns become popular, but the stitches remain the same. Learning to knit is not difficult, and you only need to master a few basic stitches and techniques — plain (knit) and purl, casting on and casting off, and keeping the tension even — to be well on your way to making inspired projects. If you are an absolute beginner and know a knitter, ask for a little help at first. Holding the needles and moving the wool at the same time can seem hard, but become simple when you're shown how.

You can pick up a knitting project whenever you have a few free minutes — just remember to finish the row you're on before you put it down. You'll find that simple designs and patterns don't need a great deal of concentration. With a basic level of competence, knitting a cushion cover or a throw rug is just as easy as knitting a scarf — it just takes a little more time and more wool. Chunky knits using thick wool and large knitting needles give quick, satisfying results.

TIPS FOR KNITTERS

Keep everything you need for a particular knitting project together in a basket or box. If you're taking your knitting outside the home, just pack what you need for the stage that you're at. You don't need to buy an expensive knitting bag — a durable plastic bag or shopping bag will work just as well.

Always knit a tension square to determine the correct size needle to use. Using a smaller needle will reduce the size of the stitches for loose knitters, and tight knitters should go to a larger needle size.

Finish your row before putting knitting down. Knitting is not something you'll finish in one go, but make sure you complete a full row of stitches before you put it down. Otherwise the stitch you stop at will stretch, and you may end up with an unsightly hole or large loop.

Buy enough wool to finish the project. Dye lots vary in shade, and wool seems to show more variation when knitted into the finished product than you would think from looking at it on the shelf. Buying wool in several batches is really not worth the risk, unless you are working in stripes, when any variation becomes less noticeable.

When starting a new ball of wool pull the thread from the inside. This will prevent the ball from rolling around, and the wool will be released more evenly. Gently take hold of a strand from as close to the centre of the ball as possible, and pull it out gently. The ball will unravel from the inside. There is no need to take the wool band off.

Don't push the needles through the ball of wool when you put your knitting down. As the needles are pushed through the strands of wool, they can separate and tear the wool fibres.

When sewing up knitting, use the same thread that it's knitted in. That way you won't see the sewing stitches. If the wool isn't suitable for this purpose, for example because it's breakable or very chunky, use a plain 8 ply wool in a matching colour.

Use bamboo skewers when joining together large pieces of chunky knits. It is difficult to pin knits together using small dressmaker's pins. Lightly sand some bamboo skewers so there are no jagged edges to catch and pull the threads on the wool. Cut the skewers in half with a pair of kitchen scissors or secateurs. Feed the bamboo pins through the knitting in between the stitches, not through the strands of wool, to hold the pieces of knitting together for sewing.

Leftover wool can always be knitted into blanket squares, or given to charities.

ABBREVIATIONS

beg = begin/ning

cm = centimetre/s

K = knit

P = purl

patt = pattern

rep = repeat

st/s = stitch/es

cont = continue

stocking st = knit right-side rows, purl wrong-side rows

MC = main colour

CC = contrast colour

KNIT A TENSION SQUARE FIRST TO DETERMINE THE CORRECT NEEDLE SIZE

USE SHORTENED BAMBOO SKEWERS INSTEAD OF PINS ON BULKY KNITTING

KNITTED CUSHION COVERS

Oversized knitted cushion covers are robust, casual and comfortable. They can be thrown down on the floor, the kids can be rough with them without fear of damaging them, and they are easy to throw into the car along with a picnic rug and a hamper of sandwiches.

With no textural pattern to follow, the covers are easy to knit. They are made up of two striped squares 58 cm x 58 cm (23 in x 23 in) knitted in stocking stitch, changing colours every 12 rows. They can be knitted in any colours, and the stripes can be any width. We used Cleckheaton Country wool.

Cushion inserts with soft, light fillings are best suited to the loose fit of the covers. They are easy to stitch up with leftover wool and a wool needle. To wash the cushions, just unpick a few of the seam stitches, pull out the insert and wash the covers by hand. (Keep leftover wool for stitching the cover back up after washing.)

Tension This handknit has been designed at a tension of 22 stitches and 30 rows to 10 cm (4 in) over stocking stitch, using 4.00 mm needles.

STEP 2

STEP 3

STEP 4

STEP 1   Using 4.00 mm needles and MC, cast on 130 sts. Work 12 rows stocking st. Change to CC and work 12 rows stocking st. Cont working 12 row stripes of MC and CC until work measures 58 cm (23 in) from beg, ending with a purl row. Cast off. Repeat to make the other side of the cushion.

STEP 2   Pin the two pieces of the cushion together, with the right sides facing inside. Stocking stitch tends to roll, so place the pins quite close together. Use pins with a round, bead-like head to prevent them from slipping through. Use backstitch to sew three sides together. On the fourth side, leave an opening to insert the cushion.

STEP 3   Insert the cushion, laying it flat and filling out all the corners of the cover.

STEP 4   Using whip stitch, close the opening.

YOU will need.

12 balls of 8 ply wool (50 g balls), 6 balls each of two different colours

One pair of 4.00 mm knitting needles (or the required size to give correct tension)

Dressmaker's pins

Wool needle for sewing seams

58 cm (23 in) square cushion insert

KNITTED THROW RUG

It doesn't take long to knit a warm blanket, knee rug or throw rug in chunky wool. Knitting a large piece can be difficult — it can get very cumbersome to handle as the knitting becomes bulkier. Knitting smaller squares and joining them together is a more practical approach that makes the project easier to manage and more transportable.

For this project, you'll need to use a super bulky yarn. It's knitted in basket stitch, which gives a look similar to basket weaving. This stitch also gives the throw a satisfying weight. Unlike stocking stitch, basket stitch doesn't roll at the edges, so it doesn't need a band or border knitted on.

The finished throw measures 150 cm x 150 cm (5 ft x 5 ft), knitted in four squares and sewn together using mattress stitch. (For instructions for mattress stitch, see any basic knitting instruction book.) As with most types of patchwork, keep the squares the same size for a neat, even finish.

Tension This handknit has been designed at a tension of 11 stitches and 17 rows to 10 cm (4 in) over pattern, using 10.00 mm needles.

STEP 1

STEP 2

STEP 4

STEP 1   Using 10.00 mm needles, cast on 82 sts.

STEP 2   1st row: K2, * P2, K2, rep from * to end.
2nd row: P2, * K2, P2, rep from * to end.
3rd row: As 2nd row.
4th row: As 1st row.
Last 4 rows form patt. Rep patt until work measures 75 cm (29½ in) from beg, ending with a 4th row. Cast off.

STEP 3   Repeat step 2 three times to make the other three squares.

STEP 4   Sew the squares together. We recommend using mattress stitch in plain yarn to sew up your knitting invisibly. When sewing up a big project like this, it's a good idea to rest it on a table. This will make it easier to keep the stitches neat and consistent.

YOU WILL NEED.

34 balls of wool (100 g balls)

One pair of 10.00 mm knitting needles (or the required size to give correct tension)

Plain yarn for sewing seams

Wool needle

PAINT

Just about any surface, large or small, can be painted, and you needn't be limited to painting walls and interiors. Painting is an enjoyable way to transform a tired piece of furniture, recycle a terracotta pot, update a cupboard, or change bathroom tiles for the better.

The paint palette is an endless spectrum of warm and cool colours, from soft, subtle tints to strong and bold hues. Specialist paints are available for all kinds of surfaces, and come in many finishes including pearl, stainless steel, rust and copper. And of course there are many ways to apply the paint, such as sponging, rag rolling or French wash.

A practical advantage is that paint serves to protect the surface to which it is applied. It stops timber from drying out and rotting, and metal from rusting. A regularly painted timber house will withstand the elements and remain in good condition for many years.

There are a few rules to follow, but these will simply enable you to better enjoy the real fun of painting — putting on the colour!

PAINTS AND PREPARATION

A little patience and preparation will go a long way to keeping your painted surfaces looking good. If you prepare the surface well, the painted surface will show fewer signs of aging. When it comes to putting the paint on, stir thoroughly first, avoid drips and runs, and paint with a light, even hand.

SANDING AND USING UNDERCOAT

For new or unpainted surfaces, a light sanding will help to remove any gunk, smooth over any bumps, and rough the surface slightly to give the paint something to stick to. If the surface has been painted previously, remove any loose flaking paint with a scraper before sanding.

Undercoat helps to bond the paint to the surface. When applied evenly, it will also help to smooth any rough patches.

WHAT PAINT WHERE?

Acrylic paint is suitable for most projects. It is available in gloss and matt, is easy to apply, and is the easiest to clean up.

Acrylic paint has a relatively short drying time, compared to enamel paint. However, it does take some time to harden, and until it hardens is susceptible to scratching.

Enamel paints are hard wearing, but generally are only available in gloss finish. Enamel paint takes longer to dry — up to 24 hours — and longer to harden. The paint is also more difficult to clean up. Enamels are not water-based, and you'll need mineral turpentine for the clean-up.

However, enamel gloss paint is tougher wearing and creates a more protective surface. It will also stand up better to seasonal changes and harsh weather conditions. It is suitable for most kinds of metal and often contains a rust inhibitor.

HANDY HINT.

You'll usually need to use two coats of paint when painting over similar colours. When painting a dark colour over a light undercoat, you'll need three or four coats to get sufficient cover. A tinted undercoat will help minimise the number of coats needed for a darker colour.

Milk paint and lime wash have a beautiful soft finish and are suitable for surfaces that are not subject to wear and tear. They come in a limited colour range, and are not available in satin and gloss finishes.

BE SURE TO REST THE CAN ON A LEVEL SURFACE BEFORE OPENING

STIR PAINT RATHER THAN SHAKING IT, TO AVOID CREATING AIR BUBBLES

SCRAPE PAINT FROM THE STIRRER BACK INTO THE TIN

HANDLING PAINT

Paint is available in sample pots, 500 ml (1 pint), 1 litre (1 quart) or 4 litre (1 gallon) tins. When ready to use the paint, don't shake the can. This can create air bubbles, which are unsightly on the painted surface.

If you are painting a small project and only need a small amount of paint, pour the required amount into a smaller container. This will minimise the risk of all the paint going off. When exposed to the air for long periods, paint starts to dry out, becoming unusable. Replace lids tightly to prevent air from ruining leftover paint.

Lift the lid using the correct tool. Don't use screwdrivers or kitchen knives on paint tin lids, as they will be damaged. What's worse, it's dangerous — a knife tip can easily break, sending chips of metal flying.

When stirring paint, you need to use a flat-bottomed tool that will scrape the sediment at the bottom and mix it with the paint. A metal paint stirrer or a similarly shaped stick also allows you to stir the paint without mixing in air bubbles.

Paint generally needs a really thorough stir, not just a couple of rounds. Stir for a few minutes in a round-and-round motion, keeping the stirrer on or close to the bottom of the tin. Change direction frequently. Don't be tempted to slop in air bubbles, as they tend to stay in the paint.

WHEN PAINT SPILLS

If paint is spilt onto any surface, scoop up as much paint as possible, rather than trying to mop it up with cloths or rags. Mopping will just spread the paint and make the clean-up more difficult.

Use an old metal spoon or something similar to scoop up as much paint as you can. Discard the paint, rather than putting it back into the container, as it will have collected dirt and dust, which you don't want ending up on the project.

If you are using large quantities of paint, a good precaution is to pour some off into a smaller container. If the container is accidentally knocked over, less paint will spill, and you'll have a smaller clean-up on your hands.

SPRAY PAINT TIPS

If you are using spray paint in an enclosed area, cover all surfaces. You should also wear a mask and goggles and if you suffer from any skin disorders, or simply have sensitive skin, wear gloves.

If a spray can's nozzle is left uncleaned after use, the paint will harden inside it. If this happens, the nozzle can be taken off and replaced with another from a second spray pack. Prevention, however, is better than cure, so when you have finished painting, turn the can upside down and spray until nothing comes out of the nozzle. This clears the nozzle and tube so that the next time you use the spray can it will work.

Some spray cans have a safety cap to prevent small children accessing the can. To remove the lid, put a screwdriver into the hole and use leverage against the top of the can to pop the cap off.

The beauty of spray painting is the clean-up. There are no brushes or containers to clean. If you have used acrylic paint, any overspray can be cleaned up with water. Enamel paint needs to be cleaned up with turpentine.

Check with your local council regarding disposal of paint spray cans.

TO CLEAR THE NOZZLE, TURN THE CAN UPSIDE-DOWN AND SPRAY

A SCREWDRIVER CAN BE USED TO LEVER THE CAP OFF A SPRAY CAN

TIP. When finished, wipe excess paint from the container using scrunched-up old newspapers. Discard in the garbage.

MILK-PAINT CHAIR

A lick of milk paint can turn a shabby old chair into a beautiful piece of furniture with a soft, almost powdery finish. This non-toxic paint containing milk and natural pigments is available in powdered form. The powder can be mixed to give a thin, watery wash or a thicker painted finish.

The paint can be sealed to protect the finish, or it can be waxed so that, over time, the milk paint will wear and age to a beautiful patina.

STEP 1

STEP 2

STEP 3

STEP 1   Cut enough sandpaper to wrap around the sanding block. Use a medium grade of sandpaper first, to sand down loose paint layers, smooth over any rough spots and rub back any built-up paint. Sand in the direction of the timber grain, and keep the pressure even. Try not to round off sharp corners unless this is desired. There is no need to sand the chair back to timber — you only need to create a surface that the undercoat can stick to. Go over the sanding using a fine grade of sandpaper to smooth off the surface.

STEP 2   Apply the undercoat or sealer, following the manufacturer's instructions. Apply an even coat, smoothing over the corners and edges so the paint doesn't build up there. Leave the chair to dry in a ventilated room, away from dust. When the undercoat is dry, lightly sand the chair with fine-grade sandpaper to smooth over any rough spots, drips or runs.

STEP 3   Mix the milk paint according to the instructions. Place the powder in a bucket, then add a measured amount of water slowly, while continuing to stir the mix. To achieve a finish similar to that of ordinary paint, mix the powder with water to the consistency of pancake batter or paint. Allow the milk paint to sit for 30 minutes so that it thickens, then give it another good stir to prevent the solids in the paint from settling at the bottom.

YOU WILL NEED.

Solid timber chair

Sandpaper (fine and medium grades)

Sanding block

Undercoat/sealer

Soft brush

Milk paint

Bucket

Measuring jug

Water to mix

Paint stirrer

Furniture wax or top-coat sealer

Felt sliders for the feet

STEP 4

STEP 5

STEP 6

STEP 4   Apply a first coat of milk paint. The paint will dry to a soft, powdery finish much lighter in colour than the mix. It may look streaky as it is drying, but the streakiness should even out once drying is complete. When the paint is completely dry, give the chair a light sand, then apply a second coat.

STEP 5   Once the second coat has dried, your milk-paint chair can be finished with a coat of furniture wax in clear or lime wax. It should then be treated as any other waxed furniture. You will need to wax and polish regularly (once a month) in the beginning, until the wax coat has built up and hardened. This may take several months. After that, simply maintain the surface by waxing once every 6 to 12 months.

If waxing furniture is not your thing, finish the chair off with a clear sealer, following the manufacturer's instructions. It won't give the same patina, but it will offer the surface more protection, and be lower maintenance.

STEP 6   If the chair will be kept in a room with polished flooring, finish the feet off with felt sliders to stop them from scratching the floor.

HANDY HINT.

Milk paint doesn't last long after it's mixed, so it's a good idea to make up only as much as you need. Any leftover paint can be stored in an airtight jar for a few days.

TIP.   You only need one paintbrush for this project, but it should be cleaned between coats. Rinse the brush clean, give it a good shake and pat dry with a towel, so that you have a clean, dry brush to begin the next coat.

THE BORN-AGAIN CONTAINER

Disposable cans, tins and lidded glass jars have excellent re-use value, so think twice before throwing them in the recycling bin. Painted to look like new, these born-again containers are both decorative and functional. Grouped together or standing alone, they can be used to hold flowers, pencils or kitchen utensils, or filled with sand to stand candles in.

STEP 2

STEP 3

STEP 1   Wash the cans, tins or jars, and peel off the labels. When the containers are dry, use fine sandpaper to sand off any leftover glue that won't wash off.

STEP 2   Sand any sharp edges off the rims of cans.

STEP 3   There is no need to apply undercoat. Just paint the container with colour, allow to dry, then give it a second coat.

YOU WILL need.

Cans, tins or clean glass jars

Fine sandpaper

Acrylic paint

Paintbrush

CRACKLE AND LIME WASH FRAME

An ornate carved or cast picture or mirror frame can be transformed using layering effects such as crackle medium combined with lime wash painting. This softens the look of the frame and gives it a weathered appearance.

Choose a picture frame that has detail and is made from timber or resin, and use strong contrast colours that will show through a coat of translucent lime wash. It's a bit like viewing through a fog or a sheet of tracing paper — in the finished frame, the colours will be muted and the fine detail blurred.

STEP 2

STEP 4

STEP 5

STEP 1   Coat the frame with a liberal amount of base colour, using a paint with a consistency similar to that of oil paint. The paint needs to be almost slapped on in varying thickness. Cover all surfaces, especially the tiny details. Allow to dry.

STEP 2   Apply crackle medium liberally all over the frame. To achieve varied cracks in the paint, use different strokes and thicknesses, and apply the medium in a non-uniform way. Allow the crackle to dry for about 3 hours before applying any other coats of paint. (Check the manufacturer's instructions, as drying times can vary.)

STEP 3   Apply a liberal coat of the contrasting coloured paint on top of the crackle and wait for the magic to happen.

STEP 4   Mix a small amount of lime and water to a consistency similar to that of the paint. Stir until there are no lumps and the mixture is smooth.

STEP 5   Apply the lime wash to the frame, allowing the paint to show through. The layers of lime wash can be built up as desired (allow each coat to dry before applying the next) or thinned down with water.

YOU WILL need.

Picture frame

Base coat acrylic — yellow has been used in the example

Crackle medium

Top coat acrylic —aqua has been used in the example

Lime (pure white hydrated)

Water to mix

Paint brush

A second cheap or disposable paintbrush to apply the lime wash

PRE-FAB STORAGE BOX

Whether it be furniture, shelving or boxes, flat-pack construction is a great way to save money. This modern packaging concept enables lower manufacturing and shipping costs. However, flat-pack items do require a little time and patience to assemble, and you need to read the instructions carefully, especially the details.

Gluing the timber together as you assemble the storage box will give extra strength to the joins. It's also a good idea to seal the timber of the finished product with a clear sealer or paint finish to prevent the timber from absorbing moisture and becoming warped or damaged over time.

Once the piece is assembled, the fun part is applying the finish. When choosing your finish, consider soft, powdery paint finishes, stainless-steel paint and timber stains.

YOU will need.

Flat-pack box, pre-cut

Sanding block

Fine-grade sandpaper

Phillips head screwdriver

Scissors

Wood glue that dries clear

Cloth

Masking tape

Craft knife

Paint tin opener and paint stirrer

Paintbrush

250 ml (½ pint) multi-purpose undercoat

250 ml (½ pint) acrylic top coat colour in matt or satin finish

STEP 1

STEP 2

STEP 1   Lightly sand all pieces to smooth any sharp or rough edges. Use a fine grade of sandpaper and a sanding block, and sand with the grain of the wood.

STEP 2   Clear all the pre-drilled holes with a screwdriver or a round file of the same width as the holes. This will help the screws to go in square to the timber.

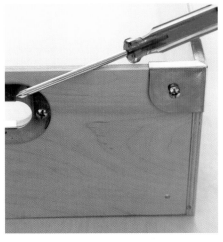
STEP 3

STEP 4

STEP 5

STEP 6

STEP 7

STEP 8

STEP 3   Use a Phillips head screwdriver to join the metal corners and timber. Don't screw the screws in too tightly, as the timber can split when the holes are close to the edges.

STEP 4   When tightening screws, make sure they go in straight. This will prevent any screw heads sitting lopsided on the finished item.

STEP 5   Smear clear-drying wood glue such as PVA on the joins and in the channels. When the timbers are compressed together, the glue will spread.

STEP 6   Use a damp cloth to wipe off excess glue.

STEP 7   If you don't feel confident about cutting in the paint around the metal edges, use painter's masking tape to tape off the metal corners — this will save cleaning up messy corners later. Cover the metal with the tape, then trim the tape with a craft knife. Cut slowly and smoothly, guiding the blade along the edge of the metal. The aim is to trim the tape so that it goes exactly to the edge of the metal pieces.

STEP 8   Apply undercoat to the inside of the box. Cut in the corners of the inside of the box first, then fill in the bottom, followed by the sides. Allow to dry.

STEP 9

STEP 10

STEP 11

STEP 12

STEP 13

HANdy HINT.

Paint is better applied as several thin coats than as one thick coat. When loading the clean brush with paint, dip the brush in, then scrape it against the edge of the tin several times to remove excess paint.

STEP 9   Apply undercoat to the outside of the box, smoothing drips and runs as you paint.

STEP 10   Allow the undercoat to dry, then lightly sand with fine-grade sandpaper.

STEP 11   Apply the first top coat as you did the undercoat. Allow to dry, then sand lightly.

STEP 12   Apply the second coat. The wet paint you are applying will probably look a lighter colour than the first coat, as paint generally dries darker.

STEP 13   When the final top coat is dry, carefully remove the masking tape.

LACE-STENCILLED STATIONERY

In a world where everyday communications usually take place via email, text messages and the telephone, there is still a place for handwritten letters — think thank you notes, or invitations to special occasions such as dinners or parties. It's easy to make handwritten letters even more special using writing paper and matching envelopes decorated with lace stencilling.

Start by choosing your paper from the array of fine writing paper that is available in both matt and pearl finishes. You might prefer to use handmade paper. Choose your paint and a lace design for your stencil. Plastic placemats, doilies or tablecloths work well, as they can be wiped clean and will keep their shape. Lace curtain material will also work, but you may need to use less paint, as otherwise the paint may soak through the stencil.

STEP 1

STEP 2

STEP 3

STEP 4

STEP 5

STEP 6

S T E P 1   Put the paint into a flat dish. You want to be able to dab the paint onto the stencil brush rather than brush it on.

S T E P 2   Do a test area first. Experiment by varying the pressure you apply and the amount of paint you use. Practise peeling back the stencil. It's not difficult to master, but you may need a couple of test runs before you stencil your final piece.

S T E P 3   Select an area of the stencil and lay it over the paper, making sure it is flat. Don't tape the stencil to the paper as the tape may damage the paper. Hold it firmly with your free hand.

S T E P 4   Dab the tip of the brush into the paint and give the brush a couple of light taps to shake loose any excess.

S T E P 5   Gently dab the brush over the stencil. Make sure you press straight down rather than dragging the brush sideways. Press lightly, and be careful not to stretch or move the stencil.

S T E P 6   Once you have completed stencilling the area, gently peel back the stencil. Repeat for the envelope and any other stationery you wish to decorate.

T i P.   A stencil brush has a flat tip and is designed to be tapped onto an area rather than brushed sideways. This prevents the paint from bleeding under the stencil, and helps distribute the paint into the intricate detail.

PAINTED SUITCASES

When storage space is in short supply, use a stack of two or three painted suitcases to store seasonal clothes, children's toys or photographs. You can find vintage suitcases or school cases in secondhand shops and garage sales and, as long as the surface is carefully prepared, most hard-cover suitcases can be painted. Look for cases that are strong, and check that the locks, catches and hinges all work.

Paint in one colour, or use several shades of the same colour, in whatever finish you prefer — matt, satin or semi-gloss. Or consider using contrasting colours such as orange and blue, or a carnival of colours for a child's bedroom.

Label the suitcases using tags or cards so you can tell at a glance what they contain. The suitcases can be stored on a chair or stool, tucked under a bed, or simply stacked or lined up on the floor.

STEP 1

STEP 2

STEP 4

YOU WILL NEED.

Suitcases in various sizes

Medium- and fine-grade sandpaper

Sanding block

Cloth or clean, soft-bristled brush

General purpose undercoat paint

Paint stirrer

Paintbrush

Rag

Acrylic paint for top coats

STEP 1   Give the suitcase an all-over sand first, using a medium-grade sandpaper. This will give the paint something to hold onto, and smooth out any rough patches. If there is any rust on the hinges or metal components, give them a light sand as well. Use a damp cloth or a clean, soft-bristled paintbrush to remove all the dust caused by sanding. If you use a damp cloth, make sure the suitcase is fully dry before painting.

STEP 2   Open the tin of undercoat and stir it well. Paint the lid of the suitcase with undercoat. Be careful not to get paint on the hinges or other metal parts. If you do, simply wipe the part clean with the rag. Wait until the lid of the suitcase is dry before turning it over and painting the bottom. If you want to paint the inside, this will also need undercoat. Wait until the outside paint is completely dry before opening the lid and painting the inside. You may also want to paint the handle to complete the look.

STEP 3   Once the undercoat is dry, sand it lightly using fine-grade sandpaper. Remove any dust caused by sanding.

STEP 4   Open the paint tin and stir the paint well. Apply the first top coat. When it has dried, sand it lightly. Remove dust caused by sanding before applying the second coat.

LEAFY STAMPS FOR LINEN

As a variation on the potato stamp, natural materials such as leaves, twigs and even some flowers can be used to add simple elegance to plain table linen.

Leaves with protruding veins are ideal for this project, with grapevine or fig leaves making particularly beautiful patterns. Partially dried fallen autumn leaves such as maple or oak are easy to collect and will give a distinctive design as their veins will have firmed up.

The designs are stamped using a textile medium mixed with paint, then ironed with a hot iron to fix the paint so that it can withstand washing. Choose napkins or placemats in durable fabrics such as cotton or linen that will tolerate a hot iron.

YOU WILL NEED.

Leaves

Textile medium

Acrylic craft paint

Dish to mix

Spatula

Sponge

Fabric items for decoration in cotton or linen

Iron

Ironing cloth or tea towel

STEP 1

STEP 2

STEP 3

STEP 4

STEP 5

STEP 6

STEP 1   Gather some appropriate leaves and place them in the pages of a heavy book. This will keep them flat and ready for painting. You don't need to wait until the leaves dry out and become brittle — a few days will do it.

STEP 2   Give the textile medium a good shake. Pour the medium into a dish. Mix the paint into the medium thoroughly using a spatula.

STEP 3   Apply the paint to a sponge.

STEP 4   Press the back of the leaf onto the sponge, trying to use an even pressure on all parts of the leaf.

STEP 5   Carefully place the leaf onto the fabric.

STEP 6   Some textile mediums need to be fixed by ironing. Always use an ironing cloth between the iron and the paint. Use the hottest temperature setting the fabric can withstand, and no steam. Place the iron down, leave it for just a couple of seconds, then lift it up again. Don't move the iron around while it's down.

TIP.   Use this technique to decorate paper items such as greeting cards, wrapping paper and envelopes.

UPHOLSTERED FOLDING CHAIR

Folding chairs are practical and take up little storage space. You can turn a shabby old chair into a chic piece that can be pulled out when extra seating is needed.

The chair used in this project was sadly neglected, but was in solid condition. The only repair needed was the replacement of a missing screw.

A humble tea towel was used to cover the seat, and a candy-striped napkin used to cover the back of the chair. There are only four screws holding the seat in place, and it is a fairly straightforward task to stitch the cover to the seat. Using fabric that is already cut and hemmed makes the task even simpler. The tea towel is durable and can be removed easily if you wish to wash it or replace it.

Metal furniture is not difficult to freshen up. If there is only a small amount of rust, it is fairly simple to sand, treat and paint. And two coats of spray paint will work wonders, with minimum effort for maximum result.

YOU will need.

Chair

Screwdriver

WD40 lubricant

Bucket of hot water and detergent

Scrubbing brush

Medium-grade sandpaper

Cloth

Spray paint with rust inhibitor

Drop sheet

Tea towel and napkin or similar fabric

Darning needle

Heavy-duty or linen thread

STEP 1

STEP 2

STEP 1   Undo all the screws. If the screws are tight or rusted at all, spray lightly with WD40, which is available at hardware stores. It acts as a lubricant and will help to loosen tight screws.

STEP 2   Remove the padded back and seat from the chair and put to one side. You will have time to work on these while waiting for the spray paint to dry.

STEP 3

STEP 4

STEP 5

STEP 6

STEP 7

STEP 8

STEP 3   Scrub the metal with hot water and detergent to remove dirt and grime.

STEP 4   When the chair frame is dry, use medium-grade sandpaper to sand the metal. This will remove light rust and flaking paint, and create a surface for the paint to stick to.

STEP 5   Wipe the chair down with a damp cloth to remove all sanding debris.

STEP 6   For heavy rust, use a metal primer before applying the top coat. For light rust, use a spray paint that includes a rust inhibitor. Shake the paint can well and spray the chair. Allow to dry.

STEP 7   Wipe the seat down with detergent and hot water, being sure to remove all grease, oil and grime. Allow to dry.

STEP 8   Lay the tea towel face down, then position the seat face down in the middle of the tea towel.

TIP.   As you remove the screws, place them straight into a labelled jar or container so that none are misplaced.

STEP 9

STEP 10

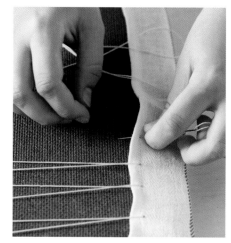
STEP 11

STEP 12

STEP 13

STEP 14

STEP 9 Fold the two opposite sides of the tea towel across the back of the seat.

STEP 10 Measure approximately how much thread you will need to hand stitch the cover on.

STEP 11 Thread the darning needle and knot the end to stop it from slipping. Commence sewing at one end, taking the needle from side to side, and keeping the tension even.

STEP 12 Finish off with a double stitch, looping the thread through the last stitch.

STEP 13 Fold over the ends of the tea towel. As before, first measure appoximately how much thread you'll need. Make a knot in the end of the thread to stop it slipping. Start at one end and stitch the ends of the tea towel together, taking the thread from side to side and keeping the tension even.

STEP 14 Neatly wrap the back of the chair in the napkin and use slipstitch to fasten the napkin in place. Make sure that the corners are neat, and that seams are not visible from the front.

STEP 15 Reassemble the chair.

PAINTED HATBOX

Cardboard or papier-mâché boxes are sturdy, stackable and great for storage. They're available in all shapes and sizes from craft shops, and are easy to paint or cover in your own design using paper, fabric, wallpaper or craft paint.

    Avoid using watery paint or glue, as cardboard tends to absorb liquid and will warp or bubble. Use a brush or sponge to apply the paint. If you want to experiment with techniques first, turn the box upside down and use the bottom of the box.

    Once you have the colour and the image on, give the whole box an aged finish with dark shoe polish.

YOU WILL NEED.

Gesso primer or undercoat

Paintbrush or sponge

Top colour in acrylic craft paint

Image to glue on the front

Craft glue that dries clear or good quality glue stick

Black shoe polish

Stiff-bristled brush

Soft, lint-free polishing cloth

STEP 1

STEP 2

STEP 3

STEP 4

STEP 5

HANdy HiNt.

If you are using dark or strong colours, starting with a dark undercoat or gesso will give a rich base to build colour on, and stop the white from showing through. It will also prevent the cardboard from absorbing the paint.

STEP 1   If you are using a dark top coat, give the box an all-over coat of undercoat or gesso in black. Paint inside the rim of the box and the lid. Allow to dry thoroughly.

STEP 2   Apply an even top coat using a brush or sponge. Allow to dry, then apply a second coat.

STEP 3   When the second coat is dry, glue the picture to the front of the box. Examples of images you could use include the cover of an old magazine or a page of sheet music. Apply a thin coat of glue to the back of the picture with a brush. Don't allow the

glue to soak the paper, as that will cause it to shrink and wrinkle as it dries. Wait until the glue becomes tacky before applying the image to the box. You can also use a good quality glue stick to hold the image in place.

STEP 4   Add an aged finish to the box and the image using shoe polish. Apply the polish in patches with a stiff-bristled brush and use irregular strokes to achieve an uneven, patchy finish.

STEP 5   Use a soft, lint-free cloth to buff the box. Depending on the polish used, it will buff to a matt or gloss shine.

GLUE

A dab of glue can turn an object tucked away in a cupboard into a beautiful, decorative item in no time at all. For example, take something as ordinary as a plain photo frame, cover it with shells collected while away at the beach, and you have a beautiful memento in which to frame a favourite holiday photo.

Glue is a simple and easy medium to use, and requires little skill — just some care when handling. All you need to do is select the right glue (see page 130, which details different kinds of glues, and their uses), and detailed instructions are generally included on the packaging. When gluing, cover the work surface with newspaper or an old cloth first, just as a precaution. Some glues can be quite difficult to remove.

Glue can be a great cheat's way of adding embellishments, rather than stitching or machine sewing. Use it to attach ribbons, buttons, beads and bows. This works best when the item you are embellishing will not be used heavily or handled often.

THE RIGHT GLUE

When choosing the glue to use for a project, give some thought to the materials and the purpose, and always follow the manufacturer's instructions. For lightweight materials, use a lightweight glue; for heavier materials, use heavyweight glue that has the strength and bonding qualities you'll need.

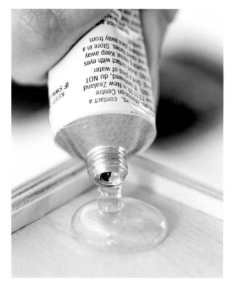

CLEAR GLUE WON'T SHOW WHEN DRY

FOR HEAVY ITEMS USE A HOT GLUE GUN

Paper Use glues that are relatively dry, such as spray adhesive or rubber cement.
If paper becomes soggy or wet with liquid glue, it will shrink and bubble as it dries.

Fabrics Use craft glue, which will hold the fibres and glue them together. Craft glue also works well for gluing fabric to paper.

Durable or bulky materials A hot glue gun will give varied results, depending on the temperature that the gun heats to and the type of glue used. If in doubt, check with the retailer. A hot glue gun can't be used with all materials — it will melt heat-sensitive products.

Wood Wood glue is suitable for most timbers and timber veneer. If the timber has been waxed, it will need to be stripped before the glue is applied.

Craft materials Craft glue that dries clear is suitable for craft materials such as cardboard, paper and foils. It is available as a thick and tacky glue which is ideal for holding on heavier items such as buttons and beads. For lighter items, you can use a more liquid consistency of glue, which allows a thinner film to be spread. Try liquid nails for a strong bond with heavier materials. Glues that are particularly suitable for ceramics and plastics are also available. Always read the manufacturer's instructions.

SURFACE PREPARATION

Glue is only as strong as the surface it is bonded to. So if you glue to peeling paint, sooner or later the glue will fall off, along with the paint it is attached to.

Before gluing, always check the surfaces for dust, dirt, grease and peeling surfaces. These should be washed clean or sanded. A very smooth surface can be given a light sanding to roughen up the surface and give the glue something to bond to.

For most glue types, you will get the best result by putting glue on both surfaces and allowing the surfaces to become tacky before joining them together. (This is not necessary when using a glue gun or paper glues.) Whatever you are gluing, allow time for the glue to dry and the surfaces to become bonded.

SAFETY

Keep glue away from youngsters. Don't inhale the fumes from strong glues — always work in a well-ventilated room.

TIP. As the glue is drying, take care that the object doesn't slip from the surface that it is holding to. You can use clips, pegs or a little masking tape to keep objects in place as the glue dries.

BUTTON TABLE LAMP

This project is an easy way to change a lamp to better suit the look of a room. Cloth-covered buttons are ideal for this project. Button shells are available from haberdashery, craft and fabric stores, and you don't need any special tools. You could also use small artificial flowers, beads, old coins, shells or feathers.

You can use this technique to decorate just about any kind of lampshade. However, if you choose to use a hot glue gun instead of craft glue, be sure to check that it won't melt the lampshade material.

STEP 1

STEP 2

STEP 3

STEP 4

YOU WILL NEED.

Covered buttons or other objects

Spatula or palette knife

Glue

Table lamp

STEP 1   Choose or make your covered buttons. If making them, use cotton, linen or light- to medium-weight fabrics. Heavy or very delicate fabrics tend not to work as well.

STEP 2   Apply a thick layer of craft glue to the back of the button using a spatula or palette knife.

STEP 3   Leave the button to rest until the glue becomes tacky.

STEP 4   Position the button on the lampshade and press it firmly into place. Allow the glue to set before turning the lamp and applying the next button. Continue adding buttons one by one until the lampshade looks balanced and complete.

BUTTON FRAME

An assortment of buttons can add great visual appeal to a frame with a wide timber surround. Collections of buttons often come up at flea markets and garage sales, or you could raid that jar of old buttons at the back of the cupboard. Use a hot glue gun to attach buttons of every size in every colour of the rainbow, or go for a more unified look, depending on what you have available.

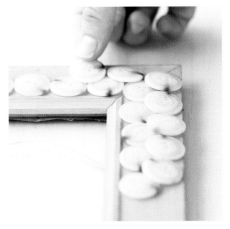

STEP 3

STEP 4

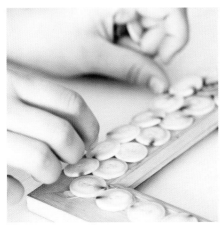

STEP 5

STEP 1   Remove the picture from the frame. If it has been put together by a picture framer, there will be staples or U-pins to remove. Use a pair of pliers to pull the pins or staples out. Remove all backing boards and the glass face and put them aside. Take care when handling the glass face.

STEP 2   Wipe the frame over using a cloth and some hot water to which you've added a small amount of detergent. (Wring the cloth out so that it is damp, rather than wet.) This will remove dirt or grease that would otherwise prevent the glue from sticking.

STEP 3   Lay the buttons on top of the frame to work out a pattern. If the frame will be standing up, make sure the edge it will be resting on is flush, so it can sit on a flat surface evenly. If the frame will hang on a wall, the design can go over the edges.

STEP 4   Use a hot glue gun to glue the buttons in place. The glue gun needs to heat up fully before you use it, or the glue won't melt and stick properly. Place a dab of glue on the back of each button and stick each one to the frame.

STEP 5   Continue until the frame is complete.

STEP 6   Clean any dust, fingerprints and smears from the glass, then replace it in the frame. Put a photo into the frame, then replace the backing board. If there are no catches to hold the backing board in place, you will need to find an alternative to the staples that were taken out. Try using thumbtacks or upholsterer's tacks.

YOU will need.

Photo frame

Pliers

Cloth

Hot water and detergent

Hot glue gun

Glue sticks

Buttons

Thumbtacks or upholsterer's tacks

MEMORY FRAME

If you have spent summers at the beach, you probably have a collection of shells or pebbles. A frame decorated with found objects such as seashells, seeds, pods or even feathers that you have collected is a lovely memento. If you don't already have a suitable frame, look in charity shops or secondhand stores for a frame with a flat front in timber or another material to which the glue will stick. Avoid frames with a lot of moulded detail.

STEP 1

STEP 2

STEP 3

YOU WILL NEED.

Photo frame

Fine- or medium-grade sandpaper

Shells or other found objects

Glue gun

Glue sticks

STEP 4

STEP 5

STEP 1   Remove the backing of the frame and any prints or photographs. Take out the glass and put it to one side.

STEP 2   Give the frame a light sanding to create a surface the glue will stick to. Wipe or brush any dust from sanding off the frame.

STEP 3   Lay the shells or other found objects onto the frame and work out a design.

STEP 4   Put some glue onto the frame in the spot where you want to place a shell.

STEP 5   Place the shell onto the glue. For shells that don't sit flat, you may need to use a larger dollop of glue and push the shell carefully onto it. Continue gluing the shells in place until the frame is covered.

COILED PLACEMAT

Make a quick and easy placemat using a length of cord or rope. Ropes and cords are available from fabric, haberdashery or hardware suppliers in many colours, textures and thicknesses — from fine silk cords to rough hemp or coir ropes. Choose a rope or cord that is flexible enough to coil tightly.

You will need to glue the cord or rope to a backing material such as suede or felt. These materials don't have raw edges that need hemming and can be trimmed easily. They can also tolerate the heat of the hot glue gun.

STEP 2

STEP 3

YOU will need.

A length of cord or rope

Felt or suede for the backing

Scissors

Hot glue gun

Glue sticks

STEP 1   To get a rough measurement of the length of cord and the size of the backing you will need, coil a length of cord to the size of placemat you wish to make. Cut the backing to an approximate size, making it a couple of centimetres (¾ in) larger than the placemat — the excess will be trimmed later.

STEP 2   Place a blob of glue from the glue gun at the centre of the backing. Put one end of the cord on top of the glue, and press it in place until the adhesion of the glue holds the cord there. Slowly work your way around the coil, applying glue to the backing material, then laying the cord over the top of it. Be aware of the tension you're using — if the cord is too tight, the placemat will lift out of shape; if it's too loose, it will be limp, and sag.

STEP 3   When the placemat is the size you require, cut the cord at an angle. Place a small amount of glue at the end of the cord, to stop it fraying. Use sharp scissors to trim the backing material.

TIP.   Don't be limited to flat surfaces when coiling cord or rope. Try wrapping a bulky rope around a planter or pot, using tiling glue or liquid nails to hold the rope in place. Or coil a delicate silk or cotton cord around a votive candle, using craft glue.

COVERED MATCHBOXES

A collection of pretty covered matchboxes can be kept out on display by the fireplace or with the scented candles. Use them to store matches or other items such as trinkets, beads, stamps or paperclips. Stack them up in different sizes in coordinating or contrasting papers.

STEP 1

STEP 4

S T E P   1   Paint the matchbox with gesso or white paint, to stop the colour of the matchbox from showing through the paper. Place the box on the paper and trace around the sides, placing the outlines of the four sides together so that the paper is the right length to wrap around the box.

S T E P   2   Use a pencil and ruler to mark sharp, straight lines. Cut out the paper.

S T E P   3   Spread the glue all over the paper with a palette knife. To avoid soaking the paper through, use glue that has the consistency of toothpaste. Alternatively, use a spray adhesive.

S T E P   4   Gently wrap the matchbox, lining the edges of the paper up with the edges of the box. Cut out panels to expose the striking surfaces of the matchbox, and trim.

S T E P   5   Protect the box with several coats of clear sealer (this is thicker than timber sealer). Allow it to dry between coats.

YOU will need.

Matchboxes

White gesso or thick white paint

Paintbrush

Coloured papers

Pencil

Ruler

Craft scissors or craft knife

Craft or paper glue

Palette knife

Clear sealer in gloss or matt

DISPLAY

Varying the everyday objects that you have on display can give your home a refreshing lift. It could be as simple as adding an indoor plant or a flower arrangement to brighten up a dark corner.

Using what you have around the home, and a little inspiration, you can create an ever-changing display that evolves with the seasons. In winter, use the heavier throw on the lounge. Hand knits and visual arrangements in autumnal colours will also add warmth. In summer, throw the windows open. Allow a breeze to drift through, and fill your home with cool colours. Adjusting our homes to the seasons can help create a soothing visual space that also supports harmony within ourselves.

It is too easy to become accustomed to the way our homes look and miss the opportunity to make the most of them by adding visual detail. Take the time to walk through your home, noticing what could be changed, softened, removed or repositioned. Small changes often make a big difference, and paying attention to how your home presents visually is the first step.

TABLE CENTREPIECE

A creatively presented plant can make a wonderful table centrepiece — a beautiful, longer-lasting alternative to cut flowers. Make a statement by using plants in vibrant colours and interesting shapes in a striking container. In the project featured here, lime green moss contrasts well with the pink fuchsia flowers, while also holding the potting mix in place.

Many plants thrive indoors, but you can also enjoy outdoor plants in an indoor display — just move them outside for a few days if they're not getting much light. Some plants are only in flower for short bursts and can be put outside when the blooms are finished. Other plants with interesting foliage can look stunning even when they are not flowering.

Look for unusual containers, including pots that might normally only be used outdoors. To prevent such containers from scratching the furniture or floor, glue felt to the bottom, or place them on a table runner or cloth.

STEP 2

STEP 3

YOU will need.

Wire or metal urn

Wire brush

Cloth

Acrylic paint

Paintbrush

Moss

Potting mix

Fuchsia plant

STEP 1   Whether the urn is solid, lattice work or wire, painting it will give a cleaner appearance for indoors. First use a wire brush to remove any flaking paint or rust, then wipe the urn down with a damp cloth to remove any remaining paint, rust or dust.

STEP 2   Use a fairly dry brush, loading it with a small amount of paint. Dab the paint on rather than using strokes. This will allow the rust colour to show through. Use an acrylic paint, as this will allow the urn to continue weathering, while slowing down the process.

STEP 3   When the paint has dried, line the urn with the moss, making sure the moss covers all the inside. The moss will hold the soil in the urn. It will also help prevent the soil drying out and minimise the need for watering.

STEP 4   Half fill the urn with potting mix and plant the fuchsia into the pot.

TIP.   Not all pots have saucers to catch the overspill from watering, so it's often a good idea to water in the sink or outside. Use a spray bottle to mist over plants if humidity is low.

PAINTED BOTTLES

A collection of painted glass bottles can be used for a display of cut herbs on a windowsill or filled with single blooms and grouped together on a dining table. When looking for suitable bottles or jars, consider shape, size and outline. Classic shapes such as old milk bottles look interesting when grouped together, or one stand-out bottle could be placed on its own.

Spray paint the bottles on a table that is well covered with a drop sheet, ideally outside on a dry, still day, and do wear gloves and a mask. To wash or clean the bottles once they are painted, just give them a quick rinse in cold water and dry thoroughly. Don't soak them in water, as the paint will blister and peel.

STEP 1 STEP 3 STEP 5

YOU will need.

Glass bottles or jars

Tea tree oil

Cotton wool

Detergent

Rag or microfibre cloth

Rice

Cotton or linen tea towel

Disposable rubber gloves

Mask

Drop sheet

Acrylic spray paint (gloss or matt)

STEP 1   First soak off any labels. For stubborn labels, put a few drops of tea tree oil on cotton wool and rub over the label. This should also remove any glue residue.

STEP 2   Wash the bottles using a mild detergent in hot water. You will need to remove all traces of grease, oil, dust and lint. A microfibre cloth will help remove grease.

STEP 3   To loosen stubborn stains inside the bottle, place a teaspoon of rice and a small amount of hot soapy water into the bottle and shake thoroughly with your thumb over the bottle opening.

STEP 4   Use a lint-free cotton or linen tea towel to thoroughly dry the bottles.

STEP 5   Wear disposable rubber gloves to protect your hands, and a dust mask so you don't breathe the paint spray. As the paint will over-spray, make sure you're wearing suitable clothing for painting.

Place the bottle on a drop sheet. Follow the instructions on the spray can. You want to create a fine and even mist that almost floats onto the surface. Hold the can at least 30 cm (12 in) from the bottle and gently press the nozzle. Slowly work along the length of the bottle, using even strokes, up and down. To turn the bottle without touching the paint, put your finger inside the neck and twist the bottle around. Leave to dry in a dust-free place.

BOOKENDS

These contemporary bookends will support a display of books on a mantelpiece or shelf while adding a touch of style. The bookends need to have a bit of weight in them to hold the books in place. For small to medium-sized books, use a box picture frame filled with interesting pieces such as legumes, pebbles, seed pods or shells. Bookends filled with legumes look great with a collection of cookbooks on a kitchen shelf or bench. For heavier books, you may need to use a slightly larger box frame and heavier objects such as smooth river stones or fishing sinkers.

YOU will need.

Two box frames 15 cm x 10 cm
(6 in x 4 in)

Dried beans or pebbles to fill the box

Fine-grade sandpaper

Craft or house paint

Paint stirrer and opener

Paintbrush

STEP 1

STEP 2

STEP 3

STEP 4

STEP 5

STEP 6

STEP 1   Sand the box to remove any rough edges. Make sure you sand with the grain.

STEP 2   Use a clean brush to dust off any loose particles.

STEP 3   Remove the backing board by lifting the pins with your fingers, a paint tin opener or the end of a flat screwdriver.

STEP 4   There is no need to undercoat the box. Apply a coat of the top colour in craft or house paint. Allow the box to dry, then apply the second coat. Keep the box away from dust while the paint is drying. If you get any paint on the glass, wait until it dries, then scrape it off with the blunt end of a craft knife. Do this before the paint on the glass has hardened.

STEP 5   Fill the box to the top with beans. Give the box a couple of taps to help the beans settle into position, then top up the box if necessary. Don't force the beans in, or push down hard on them, as the extra pressure on the glass face may cause it to crack.

STEP 6   Carefully replace the backing board. Push the pins down to secure the board. Stand the box upright.

TIP.   If you are filling the frame with items such as seashells or seedpods, check the face of the glass often to keep tabs on where you are placing objects. Hold the backing board in place and gently tip the box until you can view the display.

TWIG TREE

Long, slender willow branches have wonderful rustic appeal and their rich brown works well with many colour schemes.

When dried willow has been soaked for several days, it becomes flexible. When it dries again, it becomes rigid, making it ideal for large woven or sculptural pieces. Bunches of dried willow branches are sold by florists and in some decorator stores. Of course, if you have access to a willow tree you can collect the branches yourself and dry them.

Choose a pot of a height and colour that will balance well with the willow. Beach sand, river sand or fine gravel placed in the pot will hold the willow arrangement firmly in place and stop the pot from tipping over.

The decorations can be a mixture of handmade and bought items, and you can also recycle previous years' decorations by adding a lick of paint and a new string. Wooden shapes such as hearts and stars are inexpensive and can be picked up from craft or department stores.

Choose one colour to decorate the tree rather than using lots of strong colours, as this will enhance the tree's simple, rustic charm. If the natural dark colour of willow doesn't suit your home, the whole tree can be given a coat of spray paint in white or silver (see page 105 for tips on spray painting).

MAKING THE TWIG TREE

STEP 1

STEP 2

YOU WiLL Need.

Dried willow twigs 1.8–2 metres (1 yard) tall

Large container with curved sides for soaking the willow

String or twine

Scissors

Secateurs

Large pot, bucket or other container to hold the tree

Sand or gravel

STEP 1 Select six or seven straight, strong twigs for the tree uprights. Use secateurs to cut them to 1.8–2 metres (1 yard) and trim off any stems that are sticking out.

STEP 2 Select the twigs for shaping into circles for the rungs. Choose thinner twigs that will bend more easily. Cut to length and trim as for the frame twigs.

STEP 3

STEP 4

STEP 5

STEP 6

STEP 7

STEP 8

S T E P 3   Place the twigs that will be shaped into rungs into a container of water. If you can, use a round container such as a large bucket or pot so that the twigs are forced into a circular shape. Bend the thin end of the twig, gently so as not to snap it. Place the bent end into the vessel, then gently push the rest of the twig into the container. Soak the twigs for several days.

S T E P 4   Test the suppleness of the twigs. When they are soft enough to bend without snapping, they are ready for use.

S T E P 5   Use the tall, straight twigs to form the teepee shape of the tree. Stand the twigs upright, holding them together approximately 20 cm (8 in) from the top. Space the bottoms of the twigs evenly around the edges of a circle approximately 80 cm (30 in) in diameter.

S T E P 6   Tie the twigs together with twine or string approximately 20 cm (8 in) from the top.

S T E P 7   To make the rungs, bend the twigs first to help to get the round shape. Start from the bottom and work your way up. Work around the tripod, tying the stems to the straight twigs.

S T E P 8   Stand the tree in a large pot weighted with gravel or sand. If all the twigs at the bottom of the tree are level, the tree can also be displayed standing by itself, without a pot.

DECORATING THE TREE

STEP 1

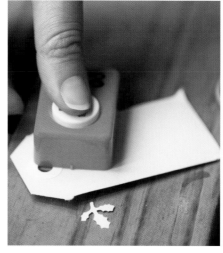

STEP 2

STEP 4

YOU WILL NEED.

Twig tree

Wooden decorations

Paint and paintbrush

Shipping tags

Punch-out stamp

Rubber stamp and stamp pad

Twine or string

Scissors

STEP 5

STEP 6

STEP 1   Give your wooden decorations a coat of paint in keeping with the colour scheme you've chosen — we chose a red theme. Inexpensive paper stars also make a simple, lightweight addition to the tree.

Extra sparkle can be added by dabbing onto the decorations some glitter mixed with clear-drying glue. Ready-mixed glitter and glue can also be purchased in craft stores.

STEP 2   Use the punch-out stamp to make decorative cut-outs on the shipping tags. Position the stamp and push down sharply to cut the through the tag.

STEP 3   Use a rubber stamp and stamp pad to add a message to each shipping tag.

STEP 4   Use twine or string to tie the tags to the tree.

STEP 5   As you add the decorations, stop every so-often and check they are spaced to your liking. Adjust if necessary.

STEP 6   When you are finished, do a final check to make sure there are no sharp twiggy pieces sticking out, particularly at children's eye level. Tuck in any loose twigs and tie them off tightly.

MINI MAKEOVERS

INSPIRING WAYS TO TRANSFORM
AN AREA IN YOUR HOME

BALCONY MAKEOVER

Start your day in harmony and peace, reading or sipping tea in the morning sun in a specially created space. The balcony of this contemporary home has a wonderful view, and is the perfect place to have breakfast, or just sit and watch the boats sail past.

In this makeover, we wanted to create an enchanting yet simple area, without making the space appear cluttered at all. The balcony has a neutral colour palette to which bold splashes of earthy colours can be added for a striking look. The balcony itself provides an almost blank canvas, so strong sculptural shapes will add definition.

The metal lace table and chairs (rescued from a roadside clean-up) are small enough to move around easily to follow the sun in winter and the shade in summer. However, they need a more modern colour to tone in with the slick modern balcony. We chose a chocolate brown. Carrying on this earthy theme, some pots were painted with rust paint. Rust paint contains iron filings which, when rust accelerator is added, react to produce rust almost instantaneously. It can be easily applied to any surface, and gives a lovely patina that will continue to age, but it is not ideal for sitting surfaces, as it can stain clothing.

Using light-coloured plants in the pots and adding splashes of red to contrast with the brown keeps the whole makeover lively. The succulent plants were chosen for their sculptural shapes and soft shades of green. To soften the overall feel, a couple of cushions can be scattered and an old candle lantern lit on sultry summer evenings. A salvaged piece of worn-out floor rug has been mixed with a silk border to make one stunning cushion. Another cushion has a simple ribbon embellishment to soften the starkness of the light colour against the dark furniture.

The work on this makeover takes only a couple of hours. However, the enamel spray paint will take at least overnight to dry, and you will need two coats to protect the metal from rusting. You also need to allow about an hour to wash the dirt and grime off the metal furniture in preparation for painting.

THE COLOUR AND SHAPE OF THE RED POT COMPLEMENT THE COLOURS AND SHAPES OF THE OTHER HANDMADE POTTERY PIECES

BOLD SHAPES LOOK EFFECTIVE AGAINST THE SIMPLICITY OF A MODERN BALCONY. GROUP OBJECTS OF SIMILAR COLOURS OR SHAPES TOGETHER

A SECTION OF A FAVOURITE ANTIQUE RUG THAT IS WORN BEYOND REPAIR CAN BE USED TO CREATE A BEAUTIFUL AND UNIQUE CUSHION COVER

PRESSED METAL TABLE AND CHAIRS

This white lace garden set — which could easily have been overlooked as being too frilly — has been given a more contemporary colour and used as the basis for a modern, eclectic balcony makeover.

If the furniture is to be left out in the weather, enamel paint is most suitable, as it will provide the greatest protection. Colours are usually limited to basics, but with a little thought you can make outstanding colour statements using accessories such as cushions, table runners and pots.

If the furniture is only lightly rusted, select a paint with a rust inhibitor. It will save you the time and effort of applying metal primer. If the furniture is heavily rusted, you may need to use a rust converter and a primer. Rust converter chemicals need to be handled with caution. Follow the manufacturer's instructions, then apply a metal primer to prevent further rusting and allow to dry before adding the enamel paint top coats. This all takes time, but if the table is worth restoring, the effort is worthwhile.

Spray paint makes painting metal lacework easy — and there are no brushes to clean up. Enamel paint takes much longer to dry than acrylic paint and it's harder to remove the overspray, so use a drop sheet and wear protective clothing. To remove paint from fingers, you will need mineral turpentine.

YOU WILL NEED.

Bucket with hot water and detergent

Scrubbing brush

Wire brush

3 or 4 cans of enamel spray paint with a rust inhibitor

Drop sheet or protective cloth and protective clothing

STEP 1

STEP 2

STEP 4

STEP 1   Use a wire brush to scrub over the lace table and chairs. This will remove any flaking paint and will also help to loosen dirt and grime. Remember to scrub the underside as well.

STEP 2   Wash down the furniture with hot water and detergent to remove all dirt and grease. Use a stiff scrubbing brush with long bristles to get into the lace detail. This may seem tedious, but the paint will only stick to the surface if it is scrupulously clean. Preparation is particularly important if the table and chair will be exposed to the weather, which is unkind to poorly prepared or badly painted surfaces.

STEP 3   If the metal is heavily rusted, you will need to apply a coat of rust converter and a coat of metal primer before painting the top coat. Follow the manufacturer's instructions.

STEP 4   Shake the spray can well for a couple of minutes to ensure the paint pigment is well mixed. Hold the can between 40 and 60 cm (16–24 in) away from the surface. Use a fine mist and go over each area several time to achieve an evenly distributed coat of paint. Remember to paint the underside of the furniture as well, to give it thorough protection against the elements.

Leave the paint to dry overnight. Make sure it is in a dust-free environment, as airborne dust will stick to the paint.

STEP 5   Once the first coat of paint is dry, apply a second coat, remembering again to paint the underside of the furniture. The paint will take a couple of days to harden, and will continue to harden fully over a period of a couple of months.

HANDY HINT.

Use car washing detergent and hot water to wash metal and painted outdoor furniture. It will cut through dirt, grease and grime. Don't use a wash and wax detergent, though, or any product that contains silica, as it will stop the paint adhering to the washed surface.

CUSHIONS

Adding some decorative details such as a few scatter cushions can soften the overall feel of a balcony that might otherwise seem stark. If you are using earth tones in your makeover, choose colours such as red and orange for your cushions, to retain the earthy feel and complement the browns. The cushions pictured on page 152 are very different to each other, but the colours allow them to work together.

A large box cushion works well on the floor. Filled with a feather and down mix, it is perfectly comfortable for children to flop onto. Cushions can also be made from squares cut from a favourite antique rug that is worn beyond repair. Simply sew a silk or cotton border around the rug square and you have one side of a beautiful cushion cover.

In this project, we have started with a small, pale cushion the right size for tucking behind your back. It has had a ribbon detail added, to tie it in with the colour of the furniture. We have used grosgrain ribbon, which adds a nice bit of texture with its ribbed effect.

STEP 1

STEP 2

STEP 3

STEP 1   Remove the cushion insert from the cover.

STEP 2   Measure around the cushion and add 2 cm (¾ in) to this measurement to determine the ribbon length required. Measure and cut the ribbon.

STEP 3   Leave the fastening or zip of the cushion cover undone. Decide where you want the ribbon to be placed on the cushion and mark the position with tailor's chalk. Pin one end of the ribbon to the cushion cover at the side seam, leaving 1 cm (½ in) overhanging the seam. Wrap the ribbon around the cover, pinning as you go, and continuing until the ends of the ribbon meet and overlap. Turn each end of the ribbon under 1 cm (½ in). Tack the ribbon in place.

STEP 4   Machine stitch the ribbon onto the cover. Insert the cushion.

YOU WILL need.

Cushion cover and insert

Measuring tape

Grosgrain ribbon

Scissors

Tailor's chalk

Pins

Needle and thread for tacking

Sewing machine

RUST POTS

Rust paint was used to give these pots their rich colour and matt finish. If you are placing the pots on light-coloured stone, concrete or terrazzo, and are concerned about rust rings, put a saucer underneath each pot.

Scrub the pots first with water and detergent with a capful of disinfectant added, to kill any bacteria. Allow to dry thoroughly before you begin painting.

STEP 1

STEP 2

STEP 3

STEP 4

YOU will need.

Pots

Rust paint and accelerator

Paint stirrer

Old or disposable paint brush

Gloves and mask

Drop sheet

STEP 1   If using plastic pots, use a coarse grade of sandpaper to roughen the surface. Open the paint and give it a thorough stir. The paint is thick and heavy as it contains iron filings.

STEP 2   Apply the paint straight onto the surface (there is no need to undercoat). Paint the inside too, to just below where the potting mix will come up to. Allow the first coat to dry before applying the second coat. Wash the paintbrush, and wait for the second coat of paint to dry before you move on to the next step.

STEP 3   Pour a small amount of rust accelerator into a container. Be careful not to breathe the fumes . A mask is advisable if you suffer any breathing difficulties, and use gloves if you have sensitive skin.

STEP 4   Apply the accelerator with the clean paintbrush, holding the pot over a drop sheet as you do so, as it will drip. Within a few minutes, rust will start to form. When you have finished coating the pot, put it down on the drop sheet. Allow the pot to dry before adding the soil and the plant.

$$y = (x+2)(x-6)$$

STEPHEN KING
STEPHEN KING

1:55

STUDY OR OFFICE SPACE MAKEOVER

Almost everyone over the age of five needs a computer or desk space at home. Even if you are short on space, it needn't be a major job to create a functional working area. A desk, chair, filing box or drawer and a shelf are all you need to get a home office organised.

Giving furniture a mini-facelift is rewarding, and you won't need to spend a great deal of money. Use what you already have available, or check out auctions, garage sales and secondhand stores.

A clutter-free space is more easily achieved if your overall design is simple. Keep the feel light and airy by staying away from chunky or bulky fittings and furniture. When decorating with colour, or changing the colours, keep the palette simple, particularly if using strong or bold colours. Try to stick to a maximum of three or four colours.

A teenager's study space was needed in this home. Space was available in the bedroom, which also had a lot of natural light.

A desk was brought in from another room, a funky chair was given a facelift, and a pinboard and chalkboard added. For the colour palette, red, stainless steel, grey and black have been used, without the wall colour needing to be changed. A wastepaper basket, a bookshelf, a tray for papers and a small chest of drawers for miscellaneous stationery and electronic equipment completes this simple, practical and modern design.

STACKED MARBLE DRINK COASTERS MAKE A GREAT PAPERWEIGHT

ENHANCE THE LIGHT AND AIRY FEEL BY USING A MESH WASTEBASKET

KEEP FREQUENTLY USED ITEMS TOGETHER AND IN EASY REACH

METAL CHAIR REVIVAL

This metal chair was a secondhand find. As it was rusty, a little extra attention was needed. Rust converter was used, then a metal primer applied for maximum protection against future rust before the top coats were added. (See page 105 for tips on spray painting.)

If a chair is severely rusted, or if there are obvious holes through the metal, it is likely to be beyond repair. Rust weakens metal, and heavily rusted metal can bend or break under pressure. For safety, do not use metal that has anything other than surface rust, and be sure to treat it to prevent further rust.

YOU WILL NEED.

Chair

Wire brush

Bucket of hot water and detergent

Scrubbing brush

Rust converter

Measuring jug

Metal primer spray paint

Enamel spray paint with rust inhibitor

STEP 1

STEP 2

STEP 3

STEP 4

STEP 5

STEP 6

STEP 1   Use a wire brush to remove any flaking paint and rust. Give the chair a really good rub over with the brush, getting into the corners and grooves. Wash the chair down using hot water and a scrubbing brush, and allow it to dry thoroughly.

STEP 2   Mix the rust converter according to the manufacturer's instructions. It's a good idea to wear thick rubber gloves when handling these chemicals.

STEP 3   Paint the rust converter onto the metal. Cover all surfaces, especially in the corners and metal joints.

STEP 4   Spray the chair with a metal primer. Allow to dry thoroughly.

STEP 5   Spray the top coat using light, even strokes to build up the paint. If you spray the paint heavily, it may drip and run. Allow to dry before applying the second coat. You may need to wait overnight. Allow the paint to harden after the second coat before resting anything on it.

STEP 6   Rubber feet can be added to protect floors from scratching, and a cushion will make the chair more comfortable.

PINBOARD

An unusual and functional pinboard can be made by threading the holes in a pegboard with ribbed elastic to hold papers and notices in place.

This board has been painted with stainless steel paint. Other possible interesting finishes include using a matt black or red paint and white elastic, or a white board with black elastic. Pegboards are generally available in pre-cut sizes from hardware stores.

Ribbed elastic is usually only available in black or white. Dying the elastic another colour is not advisable, as it will cause the rubber to perish.

HANDY HINT.

In addition to the elastic, you can add to the board pins and pegs from the hardware store. These can be useful for holding objects like keys and chains. They are available in various sizes, so you'll be able to find something to suit. Or you can glue wooden clothes pegs (the type that have the spring in them) to the board, paint them the same colour , and use them to clip papers or a favourite baseball cap.

STEP 3

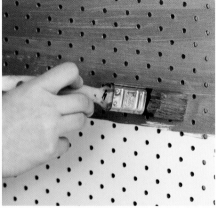

STEP 4

YOU WILL NEED.

Pegboard

Fine-grade sandpaper

Stainless steel paint

Paint stirrer

Paintbrush

4 or 5 metres (4 or 5 yards) ribbed 5 mm (¼ in) elastic

STEP 1   Lightly sand the board with fine sandpaper and brush off the dust.

STEP 2   Stir the paint thoroughly.

STEP 3   To prevent the paint from filling the holes or dripping through to the back of the board, after dipping the brush into the paint scrape most of it off the brush and back into the tin. This will give a lighter coat of paint, which will prevent the board from looking messy and make the finish more professional.

STEP 4   For a brushed stainless steel look, apply the paint in long strokes across the board. Allow to dry thoroughly. Lightly sand the board and remove any dust before applying a second coat of stainless steel paint.

IN-TRAYS

In-trays are handy for storing documents and assignments, and older style timber trays can be given a squirt of spray paint to match your colour scheme. If you are using leftover paint from the metal furniture, then enamel spray paint will be fine. It's not necessary to use enamel paint, though, as you don't need rust protection, and the enamels take much longer to dry.

STEP 1   STEP 2

STEP 1   Wipe the trays down with a damp cloth to remove dirt, allow to dry, then lightly sand with fine-grade sandpaper.

STEP 2   Rest the tray on an old paint tin or other can to give it height. This will allow the tray to be sprayed right to the edge without its sticking to the drop sheet, and will also prevent the drop sheet from getting covered in paint.

YOU will need.

Wooden in-trays

Damp cloth

Fine-grade sandpaper

Spray paint

Drop sheet

TIP.   If you have been applying enamel paint with a brush and discover at clean-up time that you have no mineral turpentine or other appropriate solvent, you can clean your brush with soap and water. Use a bar of pure soap, and gently rub the wet brush over the soap, lathering it up. Rinse often in water, and continue until there is no paint left on the bristles. Give the brush a good shake to remove excess water, and press dry with a rag. See pages 104–5 for more tips on painting.

YOU will need.

Framed canvas or MDF board

Black gesso or tinted primer

250 ml (½ pint) chalkboard paint

Paintbrush

Paint stirrer

CHALKBOARD

This modern twist on the old-fashioned blackboard is lightweight, inexpensive and fun for all ages. Made from a ready-made artist canvas, the chalkboard makes a great reminder or message board.

Ready-made artist canvases are available from art supply stores in a variety of sizes. Buy a pre-primed canvas, as it takes less preparation and drying time. If you can't get a pre-primed canvas, you will need to apply a primer and allow it to dry before painting. Chalkboard paint is available from paint and hardware stores.

A canvas is easy to move and hang; however, MDF (medium density fibre) board cut to size would also be suitable, and is more durable.

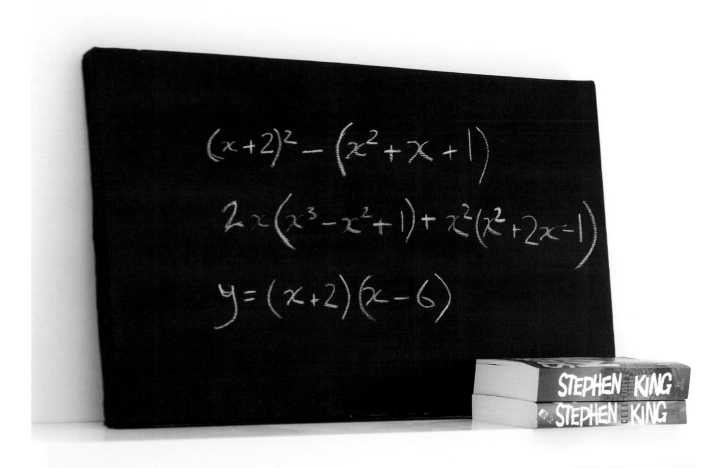

STEP 1

STEP 2

STEP 3

STEP   1   Remove the wrapping from the canvas.

STEP   2   Make sure the corners of the frame are supported, as the canvas will shrink and pull tightly on the frame. Insert plastic tabs or timber slats.

STEP   3   Use black gesso (or tinted primer if the canvas is unprimed) to undercoat the canvas or board. Paint the sides of the canvas as well as the front.

STEP   4   Stir the chalkboard paint for a couple of minutes to ensure it is thoroughly mixed. Give the canvas or board two coats of chalkboard paint. Cover the sides as well as the front, and allow the paint to dry thoroughly between coats.

STEP 4

TIP.   You might want to add a message board to a study or office space, but find there isn't anywhere to place or hang one. If it suits the look of the space, consider applying the chalkboard paint straight onto the wall.

DRAWERS

A study area needs a place to store pens, paper and general office supplies. A small set of drawers on the desktop is an ideal choice, not being too large or intrusive.

The drawers used in this project had been sitting around for a while and needed a good clean and some minor repairs. Not wanting to paint or strip the drawers, but needing to stop them from deteriorating further, a coat of clear matt sealer was added. This keeps moisture out and acts as a binder to hold the fibres of the board together. Avoid shiny gloss finishes, as this will make the drawers look shabby. Select a matt sealer that doesn't yellow, and that can be cleaned up with water.

YOU WILL NEED.

Drawers

Dusting brush (e.g. cheap paint brush)

Damp cloth and detergent

PVA glue, hammer and nails for repairs

Clear matt sealer

Paintbrush

Paint stirrer

Steel ruler

Tracing paper

Pencil

Photos or labels

Craft knife

STEP 1

STEP 2

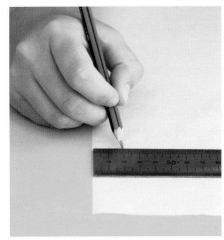

STEP 3

STEP 4

STEP 5

STEP 1   First clean the drawers. Dust them with a brush, then wipe them clean with a damp cloth and a small amount of detergent or soap. Keep the cloth as dry as possible so the drawers don't get wet.

Make any minor repairs, for example gluing down cardboard that is lifting, or nailing on loose backing boards. If you are nailing near edges, use fine nails and pre-drill a small hole. This and gentle tapping will prevent the boards from splitting.

STEP 2   Apply several light coats of sealer, allowing it to dry thoroughly in between coats. (There is no need to sand.) Depending on the condition of the drawers, you may need to apply up to ten coats. Seal the inside of the drawers too, as they are also subject to wear and tear.

STEP 3   Measure the size of the photo needed for the slot. (You can also use attractive labels.) Make sure the photo will be smaller than the slot itself, but larger than the hole that will frame it, so no edges show. Transfer these measurements onto tracing paper and draw them up.

STEP 4   Lay the tracing paper over the photo, with the outline you drew on the paper framing the part of the photo you want to show in the slot. Place a steel ruler onto the photo and tracing paper and, holding the ruler down firmly so it doesn't slip, cut along the lines using a sharp craft knife, cutting through both tracing paper and photo.

STEP 5   Place the photos into the slots.

BATHROOM MAKEOVER

The bathroom is often the one room in the house where renovations are put off. It can be a big job, costing time, money and weeks of inconvenience to the family. If you're short on time and money, and not ready to make the leap into a renovation, here are a few tricks to spruce up your bathroom.

The first step for any bathroom is cleanliness. Clear out clutter, ditch out-of-date products, and toss out anything that has accumulated grime. Give the bathroom a thorough clean, including cupboards and drawers, the sink, window frames, and the bases of taps.

Bathroom cabinets and shelving absorb moisture and can smell stale, so clean and dry them scrupulously. Use a towel rag to polish the taps and glass. Dampen a corner of the towel with tap water, polish the chrome, brass and glass, and then rub dry with the dry corner of the towel. (See page 28 for more tips on cleaning the bathroom.)

To keep the bathroom free from mould and bacteria, you need to have plenty of fresh air circulating. Leave the window open to let in air and sunshine. If the room has no windows, it may have a fan built into the wall or ceiling. Turn it on frequently, and check for dust build-up. If there is no fan, buy an inexpensive pedestal fan or desk fan to get the air moving.

The bathroom ceiling is often neglected in a regular cleaning routine, and steam and condensation can make this area prone to mould growth. Stand on a sturdy A-frame ladder or stepladder and clean the ceiling with a bucket of hot water, microfibre cloth and elbow grease.

safety tip.

If placing a ladder on a bathroom floor, always make sure there is rubber grip on the feet of the ladder. Never put the ladder on anything that will slip, like a mat.

LETTING AIR AND LIGHT INTO YOUR BATHROOM WILL LESSEN MOULD AND BACTERIA GROWTH

FOR MINOR CHIPS AND SCRATCHES IN BATHTUB ENAMEL, EASY-TO-USE TOUCH-UP PRODUCTS ARE AVAILABLE

TIP. Towels that have become hard, scratchy or frayed can be cut up and used as cleaning or painting rags. White towel rags are excellent for cleaning white walls, and any towelling is good for polishing timber, metal, pewter, stainless steel or the car.

GROUT RECOVERY

The grout in between bathroom tiles is porous, and tends to attract mould, grime and bacteria. To clean grout, use a small brush such as an old toothbrush or small scrubbing brush.

Even when cleaned and scrubbed, the grout in older bathrooms can still look tired and worn. Rather than re-tiling, which is time-consuming and expensive, try re-grouting. It's not difficult, and is definitely worth the effort in terms of how much the result will freshen up your bathroom.

STEP 1

STEP 2

STEP 3

STEP 1   Clean the grout thoroughly, making sure you remove all mould. Using undiluted tea tree or eucalyptus oil will help inhibit the growth of new mould. Allow to dry thoroughly. Scrape a little of the old grout out using a grout saw. This has a diamond tip that will give a clean line to the grout. Be careful not to scratch into the tiles. Wipe down with a clean, damp rag to remove the loose grout.

STEP 2   Pre-mixed grout is easy to use, but can be more expensive and only comes in limited colours. If you are using powdered grout, mix it according to manufacturer's instructions to the consistency of toothpaste. Apply the grout with a damp sponge, making sure the paste gets into all the crevices that have been scraped out.

STEP 3   Allow the grout to dry for a couple of hours. With a damp cloth or sponge, wipe the grout off the tiles. It is best not to leave it until the next day as the grout will harden and become more difficult to wipe off.

YOU WILL NEED.

Tea tree or eucalyptus oil

Grout saw

Rags

Grout (pre-mixed or powdered)

Sponge

FINISHING TOUCHES

The bathroom is a room that is often neglected, yet just a few special touches can make it into a sanctuary. Make sure first that the room is clean and well-ventilated, then aim to make it as comfortable and relaxing as possible.

Add some gorgeous accessories. There is a vast array of soaps available, in varying colours and scents. Choose scents you love, and colours that complement the colours of your bathroom, or bright colours to add highlights if your bathroom colours are neutral. Use natural products when you can, to avoid any reactions to chemicals. Bath oils and bath bombs can further enhance your bathing experience, and candles can be used both to add colour and to create a soft, glowing ambience at bath time. Some of the accessories could be stored in a bath tray. Make sure there are inviting towels to wrap yourself in after a soak in a steaming hot tub.

A vase of beautiful, scented flowers helps keep a bathroom looking beautiful and smelling fresh. This is the one room where more heavily scented flowers are not overpowering — try gardenia, jasmine, honeysuckle or lilies.

PLACE SMALL RUBBER DOTS UNDER THE BATH TRAY WHERE IT CONTACTS THE TUB TO STOP THE TRAY SLIDING AND SCRATCHING

AN ABSORBENT BATHMAT IS PRACTICAL AS IT WILL ENSURE THAT NO MOISTURE IS LEFT ON THE FLOOR TO CREATE A SLIPPERY SURFACE

IN THE WARMER MONTHS, USE LIGHTWEIGHT, ABSORBENT LINEN BATHSHEETS. IN WINTER, SWAP THEM FOR THICK, WARM, FLUFFY TOWELS

TIP. Sometimes line-dried towels can get a bit scratchy. To keep towels soft and fluffy, use a tablespoon of washing soda in the final rinse. Air dry towels and, just before drying is complete, give them a few minutes in the tumble dryer.

LIVING ROOM MAKEOVER

BEFORE THE MAKEOVER – NEW FURNITURE ALONE
DOES NOT GUARANTEE A ROOM WITH PANACHE

As its name implies, the living room is the centre of the house and the focal point for relaxation and entertaining. No matter the size of the room or the size of your budget, it is possible to have a living room that is both comfortable and chic.

However, simply purchasing new furniture does not guarantee a stylish and organised home. If you intend to buy new furniture, first consider the existing furniture you intend to keep, and how you might marry the old pieces with the new. Before any substantial purchase, measure the size of the piece of furniture you would like to buy, and check it will fit the available space.

Once the new furniture is in place, you may want to revisit your existing furniture and consider whether painting, recovering or revamping any of these pieces would enhance the room.

QUICK WAYS TO SOFTEN A ROOM

In this room, the starkness of the furniture has been softened by the addition of accessories using a natural palette and earthy textures. Softer lighting also helps create an atmosphere of comfort and warmth. Use floor and table lamps and candles instead of overhead lights to make a room feel more inviting. During the winter months, make use of soft daylight when the sun is low.

NATURAL COIR OR JUTE TWINES WOUND INTO BALLS CAN BE COMBINED WITH INTERESTINGLY SHAPED SEED PODS

A CRAFT STORE WILL STOCK MANY FUN FABRICS THAT CAN BE USED TO MAKE INTERESTING AND UNUSUAL CUSHIONS

YOU CAN USE BEAUTIFUL WALLPAPER OR FABRIC GLUED STRAIGHT ONTO A FRAMED CANVAS AS ARTWORK

TWIGS AND STICKS COLLECTED ON A BUSH WALK CAN BE TIED WITH STRING AND BUNDLED INTO A BASKET

WILLOW, BIRCH OR GUM BRANCHES DISPLAYED IN A VASE WILL ADD HEIGHT AND TEXTURE TO THE ROOM

SCATTER CUTTINGS OF AUSTRALIAN NATIVE PLANTS — THEY DRY TO BEAUTIFUL GREEN-GREY TONES

PAINTING A CUPBOARD

If a room contains too much natural timber, you can lighten the feeling by painting one of the pieces.
But to avoid making it look like a solid block of paint, take the edge off by not painting the top. This is
a great way to coordinate large pieces made of different timbers that don't work well together.

YOU will need.

Drop sheet

Steel wool or stainless steel pads

Methylated spirits

Hot soapy water

Undercoat

Top-coat paint

Paintbrush

Protective glaze

Rags

AN UNPAINTED PINE CABINET CAN
LOOK OUT-OF-DATE AND SHABBY WHEN
COMBINED WITH CLASSIC FURNITURE

STEP 1   STEP 2   STEP 3

STEP 4   STEP 5

HANDY HINT.

When using soapy water to remove wax, make a little water go a long way. Timber swells when it gets wet and shrinks as it dries, which can cause disfiguring and buckling. Always rub with the grain — timber becomes soft when it's damp, and rubbing across the grain will cause permanent scratching. Allow to dry thoroughly before you paint.

STEP 1   Use any leftover cardboard packaging to protect the floor from paint splatters, then lay the drop sheet over the top.

STEP 2   Don't use sandpaper or a sander to remove furniture wax or shellac from old furniture – the wax and shellac will clog the paper and build up into a hard mass, damaging the timber. Use steel wool or stainless steel pads. For refined and French-polished furniture, use a fine grade of steel wool dipped in methylated spirits. (Wear rubber gloves, as it becomes very messy.) To remove wax from rustic furniture, use a coarser grade of steel wool or a stainless steel pad. Dip the steel wool in hot soapy water. The warmth of the water will help to soften the wax.

STEP 3   Always rub the timber with the grain.

STEP 4   Apply undercoat and the top coat, allowing the paint to dry thoroughly between the coats. Use a matt paint for the top coat. Once the top coat has dried, apply a semi-gloss or full-gloss translucent glaze over the top.

STEP 5   Ready-made glazes or top wash are available from specialist paint stores, or you can make your own. To make a wash, thin down a little paint in a 50/50 mix with water. For a small cupboard you will need about 300 ml in total.

Choose lighter or darker shades, in a gloss or semi-gloss acrylic paint. You don't need to use the same colour as the top coat — try a milky white to give a white wash, or a latte coffee colour to 'age' a light colour, as shown. Apply with a soft brush. As it is a thinner mix, it tends to run, so keep a cloth handy to wipe up any drips.

SPARE ROOM MAKEOVER

A spare room is a luxury, but it can be tempting to let it turn into a junk room — it's so easy to throw the ironing, toys, broken furniture and other clutter in there and close the door. But with a little organisation and imagination, you can reclaim this area as a purpose-designed space for a favourite activity such as sewing, music, reading or craft.

In this case, the spare room has been converted into a bright, sunny workroom in which a passion for calligraphy can be indulged. It makes a world of difference not to have to drag boxes out of the spare room, work on the dining room table and then pack it all away again, and this makeover will greatly enhance Mum's enjoyment of the quiet hours when the children are asleep or at school.

The room will also double as a guest room. It features a futon sofa that folds out flat as a double bed. The set of drawers is on wheels, so can be moved around the room and used as a bedside table when guests are staying.

USE BOLD COLOURS, BUT KEEP COLOUR COMBINATIONS SIMPLE

DRAWERS CAN DOUBLE AS A BEDSIDE TABLE FOR GUESTS

THIS SET OF DRAWERS WAS MADE FROM FLAT PACK FURNITURE

MOUNTING A SHELF

Before mounting the shelf to the wall, have someone else hold it up in the position you're considering. Stand back and have a good look to check that it looks balanced. Check also that it is at a practical height.

STEP 1

STEP 3

YOU will need.

Shelf

Soft pencil

Tape measure

Spirit level

Drill and drill bit

STEP 4

STEP 5

STEP 1   First decide where you want the shelf to be.

STEP 2   Have someone else hold the shelf in position while you place a small pencil mark on the wall on each side of it, at the top corners. Have your helper put the shelf down. Measure from each dot to the floor, to make sure the shelf will be level when attached.

STEP 3   To double-check the shelf will be straight, you can use a spirit level.

STEP 4   Mark the positions where the screws will go, using the pencil.

STEP 5   Pre-drill holes for the screws.

STEP 6   Attach the shelf according to the manufacturer's instructions.

JAZZING UP A PINBOARD

With a coat of paint in a coordinating or contrasting colour and some interesting pins, an ordinary corkboard can be turned into an artwork and used to display favourite pieces of work.

STEP 2

STEP 3

STEP 1   If the board has a timber frame, lightly sand the frame before painting, using fine-grade sandpaper.

STEP 2   Give the corkboard and frame two coats of acrylic paint, allowing the paint to dry after each coat. (There is no need to undercoat.)

STEP 3   Attach two screw-in hooks to the frame of the corkboard, and string picture hanging wire between them.

STEP 4   Because corkboards are so lightweight, they can be hung without any need to put holes in the wall. Just attach small adhesive hooks to the wall, and hang the corkboard over them.

STEP 5   Use pins to attach your display items to the corkboard.

YOU WILL NEED.

Cork pinboard

Fine-grade sandpaper

Acrylic paint

Paintbrush

Screw-in hooks

Picture hanging wire

Adhesive hooks

Pins

TIP.   Make a fabric-covered pinboard by covering a sheet of foam core board that has been cut to size. Use spray adhesive to glue the fabric to the front of the board. When the glue has dried, fold the edges of the fabric to the back and use craft glue to stick them down. Most types of fabrics will work well on a pinboard — just check first that a pin will push through easily.

HANGING READY-MADE CURTAINS

Ready-made curtains are a decorator's delight. They are inexpensive and available in almost any colour and fabric. They are easy to assemble with a couple of basic tools, and will transform a room. You will need a helper to complete this project.

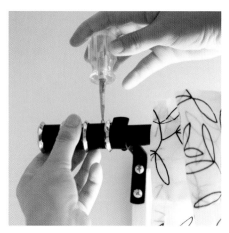

STEP 2   STEP 6

YOU will Need.

Brackets and rod

Pencil

Screwdriver, or drill with screwdriver attachment

Ready-made curtains

Measuring tape

Iron

Scissors

Needle and thread or iron-on hemming tape

STEP 1   Hold each bracket in the position where it will sit on the window frame or wall, and use a pencil to mark the screw holes.

STEP 2   Pre-drill small holes, then attach the brackets using a hand-held screwdriver or a power drill with a screwdriver attachment.

STEP 3   Measure the length of the curtains required from the bracket to the finishing point.

STEP 4   Iron the curtains before hemming them, to remove any creases and allow you to measure them accurately. Measure the length of the curtains, adding 8 cm (3 in) for the hem, and cut off the excess.

STEP 5   Turn the hem under 4 cm (1½ in) then another 4 cm (1½ in). Iron, then hem using slip stitch (see page 54).
   Some pre-packaged curtains come with iron-on hemming tape, which is also widely available in department and fabric stores. If hemming in this way, pin the tape in place, then iron. The heat of the iron bonds the tape and fabric together.

STEP 6   Thread the curtains onto the rod, then attach the finial to each end. The finial may need a screw to hold it in place.

KEEPING THE SPARE ROOM ORGANISED

The best way to stop a spare room from becoming a junk room is to get rid of any items you no longer want or use — you could give them to a friend, or donate them to a charity shop. Then make sure you have proper storage for the things you do want. Look for suitable storage furniture, for example drawers or trays for art materials. Create simple still lifes using items that look good on display.

STANDING BRUSHES ON THEIR ENDS IN A BUD VASE WILL STOP THE TIPS GETTING DAMAGED

STORING PAPERS IN DRAWERS OR SHELVES WILL KEEP THEM FLAT. KEEP WORK TOGETHER IN LABELLED FOLDERS

BRUSHES THAT ARE NOT IN USE CAN ALSO BE STORED FLAT IN BOXES OR OTHER CONTAINERS

KEEP ITEMS THAT CAN EASILY GET LOST— LIKE THESE PEN NIBS — TOGETHER IN A DECORATIVE BOX

CUSHIONS AND BED LINEN CAN BRIGHTEN UP A FUTON BED— AND IT'S READY FOR USE WHEN GUESTS ARRIVE

THE SHELF UNDER A DRAFTING TABLE CAN BE USED FOR KEEPING REFERENCE BOOKS HANDY

DINING ROOM TABLE MAKEOVER

Family time nowadays is often limited, because family members are often all on different schedules. Meal times are a great opportunity to spend time together and catch up on your individual days. This is easier if the dining table is kept clear and is an inviting place to gather around.

   Many people work from home nowadays, and often the dining room table gets called into service as a makeshift desk. It also provides an ideal flat surface for craft projects, school homework, sewing and paying the bills. While these are all valid uses, it's a good idea to make sure the table gets cleared away afterwards so it's free to be used for family meals.

   All you need to begin this makeover is a solid table and comfortable chairs. It doesn't matter what shape the table is in, or what kind of surface it has — a tablecloth or a coat of paint can always cover up any imperfections.

THE TABLE

Consider giving your dining room table a facelift with a fresh coat of paint. A simple colour change can make a world of difference. Paint takes time to harden, so give the table ample time to dry before using it for meals or placing any objects on it — a couple of days if possible.

STEP 2

STEP 4

YOU *will* Need.

Sugar soap

Fine- and medium-grade sandpaper

Undercoat or primer

Gloss paint

High quality paintbrush

Clear gloss sealer (optional)

STEP 1   Wipe the table down with sugar soap and water to remove grease and grime. If the table is waxed, you will need to remove the wax before you paint. Use methylated spirits or hot soapy water and steel wool, going with the grain.

STEP 2   Smooth over rough patches on the table with medium-grade sandpaper, again going with the grain. Then give the whole table a light sand with fine-grade sandpaper.

If the surface of the table is uneven and requires more sanding, use a sanding machine. This creates a fine dust, so wear a dust mask, cover surfaces first, and close the doors so that the dust doesn't penetrate into other rooms.

STEP 3   If the table is raw wood, give it a coat of undercoat or primer first, and allow to dry.

STEP 4   For the top coats, gloss paint is longer-wearing and easier to clean. (If you'd prefer the table to show a bit of wear and tear and age, use an acrylic paint.) Gloss paints show up defects more than matt paint does, so before you start painting check carefully that the top of the table is smooth and free from dust. Use a high-quality brush to apply the paint in long, even strokes.

STEP 5   When the first coat has dried, apply the second coat. For a more durable high-gloss finish, you can add a coat of clear gloss sealer.

TIP.   Some older tables are shorter than standard height. Adding castors will add height and make the table more mobile.

METALLIC GLASSWARE AND CERAMICS

You can change the appearance of inexpensive plain crockery and glassware by adding a simple band of gold or silver metallic paint to the rim.

Various metallic paints and powders are available from craft stores. You might find you prefer brassy and vivid colours, or the more subtle shades that are available. Consider using several different shades of gold or silver, or adding copper and brass.

As it is just the rim that is being decorated, only a small amount of paint is needed. The paint must first be mixed with a glass and tile medium, which enables the paint to stick to the ceramic or glass. When using the glass and tile medium, follow the manufacturer's instructions.

YOU WILL NEED.

Bowl for mixing

Glass and tile medium

Metallic paint or powder

Small spoon or spatula

White china or plain glassware

Stiff brush or foam-tipped stencil applicator

STEP 1

STEP 2

STEP 3

STEP 1   Place the glass and tile medium into a bowl, leaving enough space in the bowl to add the paint.

STEP 2   Add the metallic paint or powder to the bowl.

STEP 3   Give it a good mix using a small spoon or spatula. Try not to mix in air bubbles. To check the consistency of the mixture, test it on a small area first.

STEP 4   Apply the paint with a stiff brush or a foam-tipped stencil applicator, dabbing rather than spreading the paint. Leave to dry and apply a second coat if required.

STEP 4

TIP.   Metallic paints and powders tend to give slightly different effects. To find out which you prefer, experiment first with both. Powders tend to be a little more expensive and give a more subtle result.

TABLE CENTREPIECE

A living centrepiece of plants in painted pots is simple to make and long-lasting. Use plants that will grow in the garden as well as indoors, so that when you tire of them as table decoration, they can be put outside to flourish.

Paint the pots in keeping with the metallic theme, using craft or house paints. In this case, choose colours that are not too brassy, to avoid your display looking like Christmas decorations. Use terracotta pots rather than glazed pots, as the paint will stick to them better. Being porous, the terracotta will also absorb the paint slightly, giving a softer finish.

Resting the pots on tiles or trivets will stop any dampness from the pot from damaging the table.

YOU WILL NEED.

Metallic paint (a sample pot of house paint will be enough)

Paintbrush

Three pots

Three tiles

Felt

Scissors

Paintbrush for spreading glue

PVC or craft glue

Three succulents or other plants of your choice

STEP 1

STEP 2

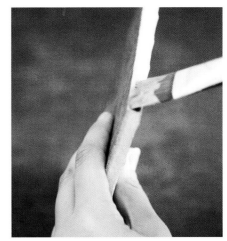

STEP 3

STEP 4

STEP 6

STEP 7

STEP 1   Stir the paint thoroughly.

STEP 2   Paint the pots, including the inside of the top third of the pot.

STEP 3   Paint the edges of the tiles.

STEP 4   Cut felt for the bottom of the tiles. This will prevent the tiles from scratching the surface they rest on. Lay the tile on the felt and mark to size with a soft lead pencil. Cut the felt using sharp scissors.

STEP 5   Place the felt against the tile and trim any excess. You want the felt to sit just inside the frame of the tile.

STEP 6   Use a paintbrush to spread the glue over the back of the tile. Then lay the felt down onto the back of the tile, smoothing out any wrinkles.

STEP 7   Following the same basic procedure in steps 4 and 5, cut felt for the bottom of the pots. Before gluing the felt to the pot, check where the drainage hole in the pot is, and cut a hole in the felt to match.

STEP 8   Add the soil and plants to the pots.

INDEX

First published in 2008 by Murdoch Books Pty Limited

Murdoch Books Australia
Pier 8/9, 23 Hickson Road
Millers Point NSW 2000
Phone: +61 (0) 2 8220 2000 Fax: +61 (0) 2 8220 2558
www.murdochbooks.com.au

Murdoch Books UK Limited
Erico House, 6th Floor
93–99 Upper Richmond Road,
Putney, London SW15 2TG
Phone: +44 (0) 20 8785 5995
Fax: +44 (0) 20 8785 5985
www.murdochbooks.co.uk

National Library of Australia Cataloguing-in-Publication Data

Stubbs, Sue, 1959– .
An hour at home.

Includes index.
ISBN 978 1 74045 899 3 (pbk).

1. Housekeeping. 2. House cleaning. 3. Dwellings –
Maintenance and repair. 4. Home economics. I. Title.

640

A catalogue record for this book is available from the British
Library.

Chief Executive: Juliet Rogers
Publishing Director: Kay Scarlett

Project manager: Tricia Dearborn
Editors: Tricia Dearborn and Anna Fern
Design concept: Sarah Odgers
Designer: Susanne Geppert
Production: Monique Layt

Colour reproduction by Colour Chiefs, Australia.
Printed by 1010 Printing International Limited in 2008.
Printed in China.

Text © Sue Stubbs 2008
Design © Murdoch Books Pty Ltd 2008
Photography © Sue Stubbs 2008

The author would like to acknowledge the following companies,
whose generosity assisted in the production of this book:
Cleckheaton yarns (for supplying the yarns and knitting the
projects — www.cleckheaton.biz); Porter's Paints
(www.porterspaints.com.au); Matisse (for art paints —
www.matisse.com.au); Wattyl (for spray paints —
www.wattyl.com.au); and Janome (for the use of a sewing
machine — www.janome.com.au).

Readers of this book should understand that this work is
necessarily of a general nature and cannot be a substitute for
appropriate professional advice.